SUBHANKAR BANERJEE   STEVEN KAZLOWSKI   HUGH ROSE   MICHIO HOSHINO   ARTHUR MORRIS

BIRDS *of the* ARCTIC NATIONAL WILDLIFE REFUGE

ARCTIC WINGS

Edited by STEPHEN BROWN   *Foreword* JIMMY CARTER   *Introduction* DAVID ALLEN SIBLEY

MARK WILSON   JEFF FAIR   FRAN MAUER   WAYNE R. PETERSEN   DENVER HOLT   DEBBIE MILLER   FRANK KEIM
ROBERT THOMPSON & SARAH JAMES   STAN SENNER   KENN KAUFMAN   CYNTHIA D. SHOGAN

THE MOUNTAINEERS BOOKS, SEATTLE ■ MANOMET CENTER FOR CONSERVATION SCIENCES

The Mountaineers Books is the nonprofit publishing arm of The Mountaineers Club, an organization founded in 1906 and dedicated to the exploration, preservation, and enjoyment of outdoor and wilderness areas.

Manomet Center for Conservation Sciences' mission is to conserve natural resources for the benefit of wildlife and human populations. Through research and collaboration, Manomet builds science-based, cooperative solutions to environmental problems.

Editor: Christine Clifton-Thornton
Acquiring Editor: Helen Cherullo
Director of Editorial and Production: Kathleen Cubley
Designer: Ani Rucki
Map design: Rose Michelle Tavernitti
Map relief: Dee Molenar
Proofreaders: Elizabeth J. Mathews, Karen Parkin

Cover photograph: *Snowy Owl and chicks* © Michio Hoshino/Minden Pictures
Back cover: *Long-billed Dowitcher,* Subhankar Banerjee
Half title and title pages: *Tundra Swans,* Steven Kazlowski
Page 4: *Snow Geese,* Hugh Rose
Page 7: *Long-tailed Jaeger,* Steven Kazlowski

Library of Congress Cataloging-in-Publication Data
Birds of the Arctic National Wildlife Refuge / edited by Stephen Brown ; introduction by David Allen Sibley ; foreword by Jimmy Carter ; preface by Subhankar Banerjee.
— 1st ed.
     p.   cm.
  Includes bibliographical references and index.
  ISBN 0-89886-975-7 (hardbound : alk. paper) -- ISBN 0-89886-976-5 (paperbound : alk. paper)
1. Birds — Alaska — Arctic National Wildlife Refuge. I. Brown, Stephen C. (Stephen Charles), 1961–
  QL684.A4B49 2006
  598.097987 — dc22
       2006000865

The Mountaineers Books and Manomet Center for Conservation Sciences gratefully acknowledge the generosity of Bev Reitz, who worked for the Arctic National Wildlife Refuge. Reitz, who was an enthusiastic advocate for wilderness, left a bequest to Subhankar Banerjee for his work on behalf of the refuge. Banerjee, in turn, elected to contribute these funds to the production of **Arctic Wings** in her honor.

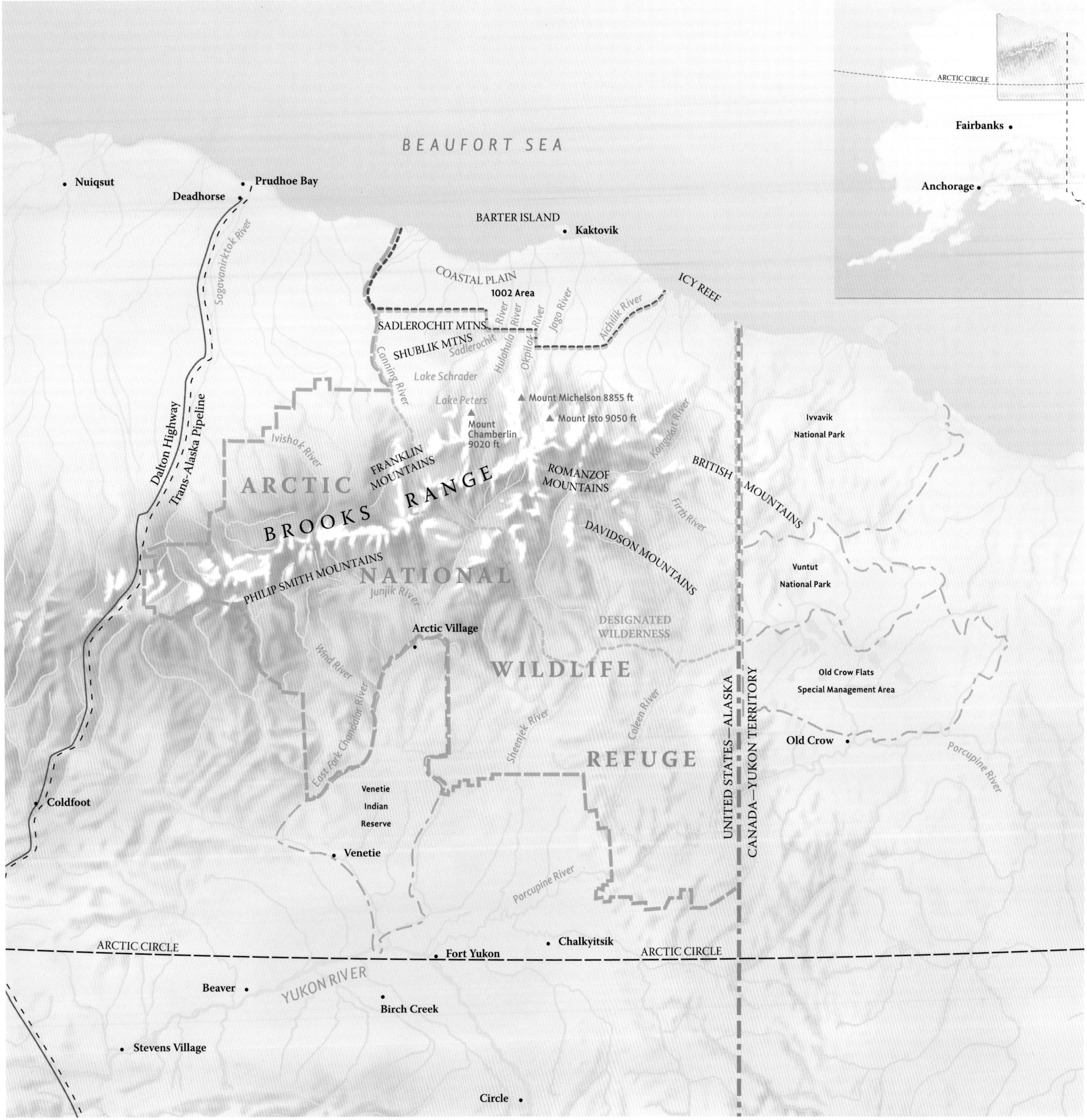

BEAUFORT SEA

Nuiqsut
Deadhorse
Prudhoe Bay

BARTER ISLAND
Kaktovik

COASTAL PLAIN
1002 Area
ICY REEF

SADLEROCHIT MTNS
SHUBLIK MTNS
Sadlerochit
Canning River
Hulahula River
Okpilak River
Jago River
Aichilik River

Lake Schrader
Lake Peters
Mount Michelson 8855 ft
Mount Isto 9050 ft
Kongakut River

Dalton Highway
Trans-Alaska Pipeline

Sagavanirktok River

Mount
Chamberlin
9020 ft

Ivishak River

ARCTIC

FRANKLIN
MOUNTAINS

BROOKS RANGE

ROMANZOF
MOUNTAINS

BRITISH MOUNTAINS

Firth River

Ivvavik
National Park

PHILIP SMITH MOUNTAINS

NATIONAL

DAVIDSON MOUNTAINS

Vuntut
National Park

Junjik River

WILDLIFE

Arctic Village

Wind River

DESIGNATED
WILDERNESS

Old Crow Flats
Special Management Area

REFUGE

Sheenjek River

Coleen River

Old Crow

East Fork Chandalar River

Porcupine River

Coldfoot

Venetie
Indian
Reserve

Venetie

Porcupine River

UNITED STATES—ALASKA
CANADA—YUKON TERRITORY

ARCTIC CIRCLE

Chalkyitsik

Fort Yukon

ARCTIC CIRCLE

Beaver

YUKON RIVER

Birch Creek

Stevens Village

Circle

ARCTIC CIRCLE

Fairbanks

Anchorage

ACKNOWLEDGMENTS

A project of this magnitude requires the commitment of countless people, and this book is an excellent example of what can be accomplished by a community working collaboratively toward a shared goal. Everyone involved deserves credit for its successful completion. As editor, I have the opportunity to thank those with whom I've worked most closely, but there are many more who contributed to this book as well. Our deepest thanks to all of you.

First, I would like to thank my colleagues at Manomet Center for Conservation Sciences who supported me throughout the project, particularly Rob Kluin and Karen Grey, who helped conceive, develop, and support the book; and Linda Damon, who finds so many ways to support our work. I also thank Manomet's president, Linda Leddy, as well as other staff who have given so much to help this work over the years, including Sue Chamberlin and Jennie Robbins, and my colleagues—Brian Harrington, Charles Duncan, Trevor Llyod-Evans, and especially Robin Hunnewell, who deserves special credit for her untiring support and hard work both in the field and with the manuscript. I thank Peter Alden and Manomet's Shorebird Friends Group for all their support.

I would also like to thank the incredible staff at The Mountaineers Books—publisher Helen Cherullo, whose cheerful support and positive attitude carried us all forward; Ani Rucki, whose capable design and layout work made the book so beautiful; and Rose Michelle Taverniti, whose wonderful maps help us visualize the scale of bird migration. Most of all, I want to thank Christine Clifton-Thornton for her mastery as editor of the project, for her exquisite skill at gently but firmly organizing the contributors, and for being a superb collaborator and colleague throughout.

We could not have completed the project without the generous support of our donors, including the Chase Wildlife Foundation, the Seabreeze Foundation, Eagle Optics, and a number of anonymous supporters.

I would like to give special thanks to Subhankar Banerjee, whose artistry and previous work have raised awareness about the Arctic Refuge with such beauty and grace, and without whom this project never would have been launched. Subhankar and David Sibley initially conceived the idea that became this book. I am especially grateful to all our coauthors and photographers for their spectacular and inspirational work, for transporting us so vividly to the refuge and telling us the stories of its inhabitants, and for fitting this project into their already busy lives of dedication to the cause of conservation. In particular, Debbie Miller found so many ways to contribute in addition to her essay, and we are all grateful for her input. Thanks also to Martyn Stewart for the wonderful CD of Arctic Refuge birdsongs that accompanies the book.

Special thanks are also due to our colleagues in the field, including Rick Lanctot, Steve Kendall, Dave Payer, and Jon Bart, and all of those who have volunteered in field camps under beautiful but also challenging conditions. I particularly want to thank Brad Winn, who used his vacation time to work on the project and helped tremendously with both photography and field work.

Finally, I want to thank my wife, Metta McGarvey, for sharing the challenges and rewards of field projects with me, for her skills as a writer and organizer, and for always supporting my dream of trying to make a difference despite the personal cost; and thanks also to my children, Claire and Ethan, who did without me so often when projects like this one took me on long journeys, and for whose generation we hope to preserve this last great wilderness.

—Stephen Brown

CONTENTS

On a mid-April day in Kaktovik, a small Inupiat village on the northeast coast of Alaska, I step out of Robert Thompson's house onto the snow-covered ground. It is cold, and the snow will not melt for another month or so. The Snow Buntings have just arrived. They seem cheerful as they sing their hearts out. Jane Thompson, Robert's wife, is very happy to see them, and so is the rest of the village. She tells me about all the different places they are going to be nesting. Buntings have brought a promise with them: "Winter is over, and spring is just around the corner." This is an important promise to a town that has been blanketed in snow for months, with blizzards and darkness for much of the time. Buntings have never broken their promise.

As I reminisce about my first sighting of Snow Buntings, I think about Terry Tempest Williams and her mother watching two white birds with black on their backs in the Great Salt Lake. Terry writes in her classic memoir, *Refuge: An Unnatural History of Family and Place*, "'I found them! Here they are . . . snow buntings! . . . I can't believe it! These are rare to the Refuge. I have never seen them before.' Mother watches the birds carefully. 'Tell me, Terry, are these birds Tolstoy may have known?'"

Robert is talking about duck hunting. In less than a month, he says, millions of ducks and geese will be migrating along the icy coast. "It is beautiful to watch them migrate in lines and formations over the ice, close to the ground," he says. Like clockwork, the pregnant females of the Porcupine caribou herd will have ended their epic annual spring migration, arriving on the coastal plain of the Arctic Refuge in time for calving. At least 157 species of birds from around the planet will come to the coastal plain, and at least 56 species will stay to nest and rear their young. Another 20 species are probably nesting here, but their nests are secrets yet to be discovered. It is a springtime flurry of activity: songbirds sing, tiny sandpipers intensely engage in courtship to attract mates quickly, Gyrfalcons hunt ptarmigans to convince potential mates that they are good hunters, Smith's Longspurs look for nesting sites . . . the drama is unfolding with intensity on the vast tundra.

Debbie Miller has told me stories of the songbirds. Few people have walked the Arctic Refuge and listened to the tundra as extensively as Debbie and her husband, Dennis. To a casual observer, the tundra may seem empty and ugly. One needs to kneel down and put ears and eyes close to the ground to see and hear these little creatures engaged in life's drama. I wasn't a birder before I went to the refuge. I knew little about their lives, but I was enthralled when I saw all these events unfolding in front of me. I made a promise to myself to give a voice to their ways of life.

In June 2001, I camped out in Sarah James's backyard in Arctic Village to attend an emergency Gwich'in gathering. The loons were calling from out on the lake. I went down to look for them; yes, they were there. Later that summer, Cindy Shogan invited me to go to Washington, D.C., where I met Stan Senner. I showed Stan my bird photographs from the Arctic Refuge. That fall, Stan produced a beautiful report, "Birds and Oil Development in the Arctic Refuge,"

which was widely distributed to congressional members and activists who were working to preserve the coastal plain from oil and gas drilling.

Summer of 2002 was remarkable. Robert and I had the good fortune to spend time with Peter Matthiessen and David Allen Sibley on the Arctic tundra. They taught us much about birds and how to appreciate their lives. Peter was thrilled to see the Buff-breasted Sandpiper; David was elated to see all these birds in their nesting habitat, species that he has been painting so eloquently for years.

Semipalmated Sandpipers arrive on the coastal plain and almost immediately start building nests. When the nest-building process is successful, the males depart for their southern wintering grounds. After the eggs hatch and the chicks are able to feed on their own, the females depart, too; now the chicks have to

Opposite ■ *Birds over coastal lagoon, Brooks Range in the background / Pacific Loon on nest*

For most of the year, the Arctic is a beautiful but harsh environment with temperatures well below zero, months of mostly darkness, and almost no visible signs of life. Amazingly, a few birds do spend the winter here—Snowy Owls, ptarmigans, ravens, and even redpolls somehow find enough food to sustain themselves in the bitter cold. But beneath the snow and ice, even within the ice itself, a profusion of life lies dormant, waiting for spring.

Tundra plants respond to the slight warming in spring with new growth under the snow. In June, as soon as the ground is free of snow, the tundra suddenly is teeming with life that will provide food for birds: Flies, mosquitoes, spiders, insect larvae, and other invertebrates thrive among the plants, and rodents are more available. But perhaps the most dramatic and visible change is the millions of birds that arrive here from all over the globe to take advantage of this abundant food and claim the Arctic as their summer home.

Although the winter landscape is barren, the summer landscape is its polar opposite, as all living things here try to squeeze the activities of spring, summer, and fall into about three months' time. In the short Arctic summer, life is intense. For the birds, it's "get in, nest, get out." The sun is up twenty-four hours a day, and bird activity continues around the clock. Some birds that arrived in June as the snow was beginning to melt have already built nests, laid eggs, and raised young by July, and they're ready to head south.

When I was in the Arctic National Wildlife Refuge in July several years ago with Subhankar Banerjee and Robert Thompson, they would often point to a particular species and ask, "Where does that bird come from?" Each time the question caught me off guard, and I thought to myself, "What do they mean?

Sandhill Crane

We're looking at a nest; that bird comes from right here." From my southern perspective, I went to the Arctic to see these birds on their breeding grounds—to see where they came from. But from an Arctic perspective, these birds are just brief visitors; some are in Alaska for only a few weeks. They may be born in the Arctic Refuge, but most of them don't really have a permanent home; they're always moving, and, in that sense, they don't come from anywhere.

Even during their weeks in the Arctic, the birds are constantly in motion—competing for territories and mates, building nests, feeding young, and feeding themselves. At the same time they must prepare for the migration south. The need for food, for fuel, is so great that even as a bird defends its nest by scolding an intruder, it will pause compulsively to grab an insect out of the grass.

The payoff for this intense lifestyle must outweigh the hardships and the dangers of the long migration, because so many birds do it. The ones that make the longest journeys have adapted physically with a very streamlined shape—long, pointed wings and tapered body—and the ability to carry large amounts of fat for fuel. And each species has developed a different strategy for migration.

One of the most amazing and well-known migratory birds is the four-ounce Arctic Tern, which makes the longest annual migration of any bird. They fly a minimum of 24,000 miles a year, essentially from the north polar areas to the south polar areas and back. They might spend three months during the Arctic summer nesting and raising their young in the north, and then take three months to make the long journey down the Pacific Coast to the Antarctic. They'll spend three months in the southern summer and then make another three months' journey back to their northern summer home in the Arctic. They spend most of their lives on the wing and in daylight. But this migration, as long as it is, is not as dramatic as the migration of some of the sandpipers.

The one-ounce Semipalmated Sandpipers arrive in the Arctic in early June, spend only four to six weeks in the Arctic National Wildlife Refuge, and then leave before their young are fully grown. They migrate southeast across Canada, heading for the rich tidal flats of the Bay of Fundy, where they gather in large numbers, building up fat. They are preparing for a nonstop flight from Nova Scotia to South America, traveling 2400 miles in seventy-two hours and burning fat equal to about half their body weight. Adults make the trip in July; the young birds follow instinctively on the same path a few weeks later.

Even though they "come from" the Arctic, the coastal mudflats of northern South America could be called their primary home. This is where they spend at least six months of the year. The Bay of Fundy, which provides fuel for their long nonstop flight, as well as other stopping points along the way, are equally important.

Sandpipers are the fastest migrants, among the last to arrive and first to leave the Arctic. Other species, such as geese and Sandhill Cranes, stay longer in the Arctic. Pectoral Sandpipers nest in the Arctic Refuge, arriving in early June and departing from mid-July to mid-August. When the first southbound adult

Examples of Global Bird Migration from the Arctic Refuge

Northern Wheatear	Arctic Tern	Sandhill Crane	Buff-breasted Sandpiper
Bluethroat	Dunlin	Lapland Longspur	Tundra Swan
Eastern Yellow Wagtail	Wandering Tattler	Smith's Longspur	Semipalmated Sandpiper

Pectoral Sandpipers reach the southern United States in July, young geese have just hatched from eggs on the tundra. By August, while the geese are still six weeks away from beginning their southward migration, the adult sandpipers already are half a world away on their wintering grounds in southern South America, and the intrepid young sandpipers are just beginning their journey south.

While the sandpipers are migrating south, geese and ducks gather at traditional molting places in the Arctic. Many species actually migrate north in late summer to molt at large wetlands where their species has gone for centuries. Some waterfowl leave the refuge to go elsewhere in Alaska and Canada; others, such as Long-tailed Ducks, come northwest out of Canada by the hundreds of thousands in late summer to rest and feed and molt in the lagoons along the Arctic coast of Alaska before flying south in late fall to winter along the coasts of the United States.

Small songbirds finish nesting by early August, and while the waterfowl are pouring into the coastal lagoons, sparrows, warblers, longspurs, and others wander the tundra, finding food and shelter in the grasses and willow thickets. Those that gather into small flocks over the course of the summer and fall, moving across the Arctic coastal plain in search of prime feeding areas, are like an unruly sea of birds sloshing back and forth at the top of the continent. Becoming more and more restless as the days shorten late in the season, first

the sandpipers, then the terns and sparrows, then the geese and longspurs all start moving south.

As autumn storms come in and crisp, cold air sweeps down across the coastal plain, north winds bring a few snow squalls and a skim of ice that edges the ponds. This triggers an exodus that sends birds southward. Like ripples on a pond that spread out from the source, the waves of birds travel south, rolling, mixing, dispersing, and converging. Some birds move quickly, others slowly, but all move inexorably south, pushed by the arctic air, each traveling according to the plan of their ancestors.

While all of this has been going on in the Arctic, the birds of the southern United States have been relatively relaxed. The climate is mild enough that many species—White-breasted Nuthatch, Canada Goose, and others—can be resident. They stay on familiar grounds for the entire year and face none of the risks and uncertainties of migration. Migratory species such as the Rose-breasted Grosbeak spend only the summer in the forests of the eastern United States and migrate south to Mexico or the West Indies for the winter. But unlike the birds that migrate to the Arctic, the grosbeaks spend many months on their breeding territories in the long, mild summer.

Some early morning in late July, a male Rose-breasted Grosbeak pauses in its singing atop a sugar maple to glance up into the blue sky. A flock of Pectoral

13

Examples of Bird Migration Routes of North America

Birds from the Arctic Refuge migrate along many different routes, and different species can be found wintering or passing through most of the Lower 48 states. Along with many other species, the birds listed here as examples breed in the Arctic Refuge, then migrate along major flyways to the conterminous United States.

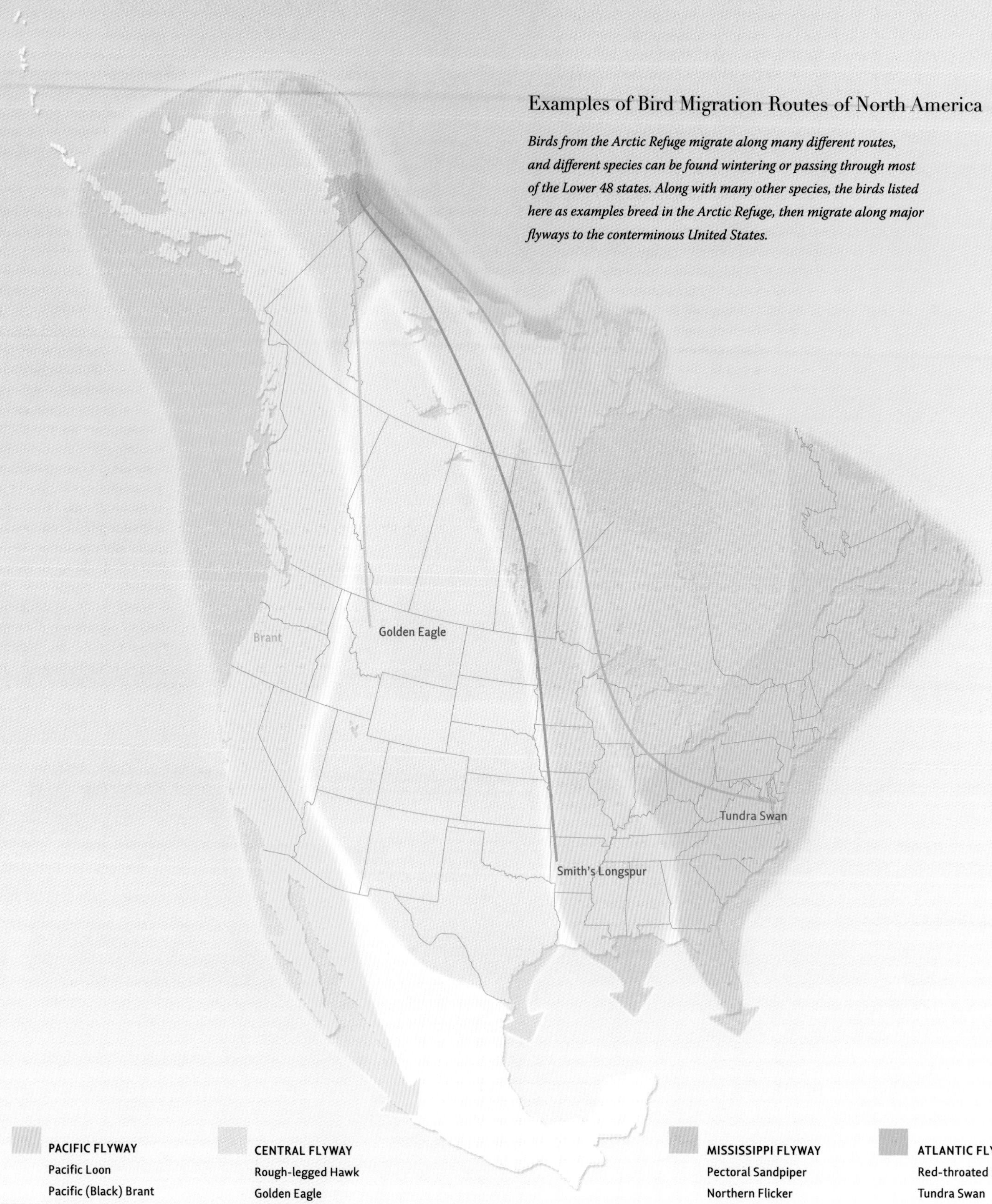

Brant

Golden Eagle

Tundra Swan

Smith's Longspur

PACIFIC FLYWAY	CENTRAL FLYWAY	MISSISSIPPI FLYWAY	ATLANTIC FLYWAY
Pacific Loon	Rough-legged Hawk	Pectoral Sandpiper	Red-throated Loon
Pacific (Black) Brant	Golden Eagle	Northern Flicker	Tundra Swan
Sandhill Crane	Baird's Sandpiper	American Pipit	Long-tailed Duck
Surfbird	Northern Shrike	Yellow-rumped Warbler	Peregrine Falcon
Red-necked Phalarope	Lapland Longspur	Smith's Longspur	American Golden-Plover

Sandpipers, flying fast and straight, is barely visible as they migrate south high overhead, traveling a thousand miles in a single hop. Between the time that the grosbeak arrives on its nesting territory in Ohio in April and the time it leaves in September to fly to Mexico, the Pectoral Sandpipers have flown from Argentina to the Arctic, nested, and flown back to Argentina.

This grand dance is passed on instinctively from generation to generation, shaped by climate, geography, tradition, and evolution, and choreographed by weather. Birds pass us by, mysterious and seemingly without effort; one day they appear and the next day they are gone. It is easy to see why early naturalists thought that birds spent the winter on the moon or hibernating in mud at the bottom of ponds.

Now that we know the routes and patterns of the birds, they can give us a sense of place, of our location on the globe. We watch them trace a line across the sky and can imagine extending the line back to where they came from and ahead to where they are going. It may be hot and sunny in the Lower 48 in July, but the migrating sandpipers bring a touch of the Arctic with them. They may have seen snowflakes and icebergs just a few days before, and consorted with eiders and Arctic Terns and longspurs. Then they come south to take advantage of the wetlands, warmth, and easy prey that they instinctively know are there.

As we imagine the migratory paths and patterns being honed over millennia, it also gives us a sense of time and history. Hearing the Sandhill Cranes migrating overhead on a cold north wind, we can imagine the same sounds filtering down from the clouds on a similar day 5000 years ago. We can imagine generations of humans before us watching the arrival of migrating birds and saying to their children, "The cranes are passing; winter will be close behind." We may not sense what the birds sense, but their finely tuned wisdom provides guidance for the observer and clues to the changing seasons.

The migration of birds such as the Pectoral Sandpiper goes back beyond ice ages. Their ancestors flew over giant sloths and rested at watering holes alongside woolly mammoths. Even the 500-year history of European settlement in North America cannot compare to the migratory history of the Pectoral Sandpiper. Our oldest cities are just a few concrete boxes that have recently appeared along their route from the Arctic to Argentina. Even though the migrating birds seem like a temporary and transient thing, and their migration a fragile thread over the land, they are as constant and predictable as the seasons.

There is a kind of music in the patterns of bird migrations, a delicate rhythm that plays over the slow cycles of seasons, the orbits of planets, the raising of mountains. It is the rhythm of the earth made plainly visible.

In many places, our modern lifestyle—with its time clocks and computers and automobiles and insulated, air-conditioned buildings and processed food— has isolated us from this rhythm. The ancient rhythms are there; they are a part of all of us. We understand them and follow them subconsciously, but too much of our lives now are separate from them, and we only hear them when we know what to listen for. It's easier in a place without automobiles and buildings and other modern technology. Sanctuaries like the Arctic National Wildlife Refuge are among the few places on earth where we can hear the natural rhythms

Steller's Eider

clearly, and where some humans still live in harmony with those rhythms.

But the rhythm of bird migrations also reminds us that even in the most urban settings, we do not really control nature; we live in constant interaction with it. Even in the heart of a city like Paris or Los Angeles, birds migrate, seasons change, trees grow, rocks erode. Natural processes are there, and a flock of migrating birds can transport us to the Arctic, to South America, to our childhood, to our ancestors. We are all connected to the earth. It responds to us, and we to it.

Nobody knows what drove the Labrador Duck to extinction in the 1800s, and nobody can predict what will happen with increased human activity in the Arctic. Oil exploration could be enough to tip already-threatened birds such as the Steller's Eider and the Buff-breasted Sandpiper into extinction. Helicopters and drilling equipment will disturb nesting birds. Pipeline and road construction will alter the delicate balance of tundra plants and ponds. Garbage that often comes along with modern human settlements could lead to an increased population of scavenging arctic foxes, ravens, and Glaucous Gulls, which will then eat the eggs and young of nesting birds, potentially leading to declines of many species. Whatever the results of development may be, it is certain that migrating birds will make those effects, small or large, visible all around the world.

DAVID ALLEN SIBLEY *began seriously watching and drawing birds in 1969, at the age of seven. He is the renowned artist and author of the extremely successful books* The Sibley Guide to Birds *and* The Sibley Guide to Bird Life and Behavior, *which set a new standard for both artistic beauty and detailed bird identification. Since 1980 Sibley has traveled throughout North America in search of birds, both on his own and as a leader of bird watching tours, and it was this intensive travel and bird study that culminated in the publication of his comprehensive guides.* ◼

One doesn't come to this forbidding place lightly.

To even know about the Arctic National Wildlife Refuge, the crown jewel of refuges, one must have paid attention to a small voice in a world where myriad media scream for ears and eyes. Most Americans, I suspect, know little of this place despite yearly spirited congressional battles over whether to allow oil drilling on the coastal plain. Few people—even those interested in exploring spectacular natural places—make the effort to get here. After all, a birder looking to jolt his or her North American lifelist would find many more wayward Asian species on Attu, at the tip of the Aleutian Islands chain, and might spend less money doing it. A mountaineer would find many higher and tougher peaks to climb in other parks of Alaska. Rafters will find better boat-eating white water on rivers outside the Arctic Refuge, and fishermen can cast more productive waters than the silty, braided, north-flowing rivers of the refuge's coastal plain.

If you nurture a deep sense of natural history or wilderness, then you will find the Arctic Refuge a moving place. Understanding any land from afar is at best a loose approximation. But consider the numbers: The refuge contains 19.5 million acres, with 1.5 million of those acres in the coastal plain and 8 million acres designated as wilderness. There are 194 species of birds that have been recorded in the refuge, with the majority—157 species—found north of the Brooks Range, on the coastal plain. Thirty-seven species of land mammals and 36 species of fish live in the refuge for at least part of the year, and more than 400 species of plants grow on Alaska's North Slope. Numbers, however, merely quantify the place; they cannot express how it looks at midnight when the sweet light lingers for hours; how sleet feels in a July blizzard when the shorebirds are brooding chicks; or how glorious the tundra smells in the morning.

The weather in the Brooks and northward is fickle and tough. Bush pilots die finding this out. Save for the tiny, isolated village of Kaktovik, roads and services don't exist. This is called *wilder*ness for a reason. Topographic maps for the Arctic Refuge most often have a road legend that reads, "No roads or trails in this area." If you come to the Arctic Refuge, you're on your own.

■ ■ ■

I and my wife, Marcia, decided to explore the refuge by canoe in search of some of the sexiest bird species a naturalist can lay binoculars on—Yellow-billed Loons, Gray-headed Chickadees, Gyrfalcons, Eastern Yellow Wagtails, Wandering Tattlers, Bluethroats, three species of jaegers, Buff-breasted Sandpipers, and thirty-five species of shorebirds. We also hoped to see Golden Eagles, American Dippers, Northern Wheatears, Peregrine Falcons, Common Redpolls, and Snowy Owls. Some of these are rare species; a few are hard to observe outside of breeding season and come to the tundra only to nest before going back to the sea for a pelagic existence.

The birds really were just an excuse to visit the refuge. More important, we came to the Arctic Refuge to gain a sense of place, to see and feel what the land was about—a place replete with predators, no roads, and few people. We came to see for ourselves what is at stake, for we, like you, are shareholders in the refuge.

Our drop-off would be almost exactly sixty-nine degrees north latitude, near the heart of the Brooks Range. Only a few refuge rivers on the North Slope offer a trip that starts in the mountains, descends to the foothills, and traverses the coastal plain with the mileage that could make for an extended trip. The Hulahula River, near the middle of the refuge's coastal plain, was one. The Canning River, on the northwestern side of the refuge, was another.

The Canning River seemed to draw us, perhaps because it cuts a symbolic course northward between development to the west and wilderness to the east. On it we would pass through three of the refuge's six ecological zones: the Brooks Range, the Arctic foothills, and the coastal plain.

We could expect to find different birds in each of the three zones. In most mountain ranges, the color of the mountains tells us what type of rock forms them. In the Brooks, limestone gives them a gray, barren presence. Sandstone and conglomerate color the ridges greenish brown. Shale can form gray or black crumbling slopes. Schist looks bluish from afar, and basalt stains the mountain a reddish brown. Plants on the mountains are scant—lichens, heather, saxifrages, ferns, grasses, shrubs. Above 4500 feet, little other than lichen and a handful of flowering plants can survive. We expected to find few birds in the mountains, although we hoped for falcons, Golden Eagles, and perhaps a Northern Wheatear.

The Arctic foothills range from near sea level to roughly 2500 feet. More plants grow here than in the mountains because the climate is less severe. The foothills get more sun than does the coastal plain, which is sheathed in fog or overcast about three-quarters of the time in summer. Tufted cottongrass, which forms fields of tussocked growth, is perhaps the most common plant found in the foothills. We hoped to see Eastern Yellow Wagtails, Bluethroats, raptors, and maybe terns and jaegers in the foothills. The foothills also are home to moose, caribou, wolverines, arctic foxes, and wolves.

As the Canning flows north, leaving the foothills for the coastal plain, it becomes the western boundary of the refuge. To the east of the river stretches the refuge's contested Section 1002 in all its complexity, a mosaic of dry tundra, wet sedge tussock tundra, and wet sedge willow tundra. Here we hoped to find nesting shorebirds and Arctic specialties such as the Yellow-billed Loon and perhaps some waterfowl. Muskox, caribou, moose, and wolverines would also be possibilities here.

To the west of the river, State of Alaska oil lease lands stretch seventy miles to the Dalton Highway, also known as the Haul Road. Built to create the oil town of Deadhorse and the Alaska pipeline, and to service large oilfields on the coastal plain and offshore, under the Beaufort Sea, the Dalton Highway is open to public travel. A week before setting out for the Canning River, we drove the hundreds of miles of the dusty Haul Road from outside of Fairbanks to Deadhorse, where we stayed for two nights in the Arctic Oilfield Hotel. We wanted to touch the warm pipeline at its source and to see for ourselves the sprawl of working oilfields, the footprint that oil extraction makes on the tundra—to see what supplying petroleum to consumers like us entails. Blink your eyes and pretend the frozen Beaufort Sea isn't there, and you might think you are in Texas. The difference in Alaska is that the oilfields are an industrial city in the middle of a wilderness.

We saw a list of "problem" bears, each named and numbered, which was held at a gatehouse to a section of oilfield closed to the public. Dumpster-diving was among the bears' crimes. For all its industrial grit, Deadhorse proved to be relatively litter- and garbage-free. The bears weren't a problem until oil was discovered; now they're criminals in their own land. Texas, on the other hand, killed off its last grizzly bear, in the Davis Mountains, in 1890.

Franklin Mountains

On a late June day, Marcia and I flew north out of Arctic Village into the Arctic National Wildlife Refuge, over the Philip Smith Mountains, and on to the Franklin Mountains. Our cargo included a seventeen-foot Pakcanoe, an amazing collapsible boat that packs into a medium-size duffle and fits easily into a Cessna. Give a photographer a canoe and he considers it the world's biggest camera bag—a floating camera bag. The canoe would allow me to bring an array of lenses, a carbon-fiber tripod, three 35mm camera bodies, a 35mm panoramic camera, a lot of spare batteries, and 100 rolls of film. For a photographer, canoeing is the ultimate way to travel, the perfect compromise between load limit and mobility. Along with the usual range of camping gear associated with isolated northern destinations, we brought Gore-Tex dry suits to prevent potentially fatal hypothermia, should either of us go for an inadvertent swim in the frigid waters of the Canning River. Our final piece of equipment was an aviation band radio, which we could use to talk to any plane in sight, be it a local bush pilot buzzing past or an international jet headed for Seoul at 35,000 feet. In an emergency, we could radio out for help or advice.

Mark and Marcia Wilson in canoe with aufeis on Canning River

JUNE 28. I wonder if migrating birds can feel awe, fear, and excitement, all at the same time. It's what I feel as I peer from the passenger window of Kirk Sweetsir's Cessna 185, a tail-dragger equipped with balloon tundra tires. Below—and at times not that far below—are some of the harshest limestone mountains I've ever encountered. As we fly over fields of unnamed peaks in the Brooks Range, the land looks big, new, and raw. No evidence of human doings marks these mountains. Most of the peaks support little vegetation that is visible from a plane. Botanists call parts of the Brooks "rock desert," a place inhospitable to plants and birds.

July snowstorm, Canning River

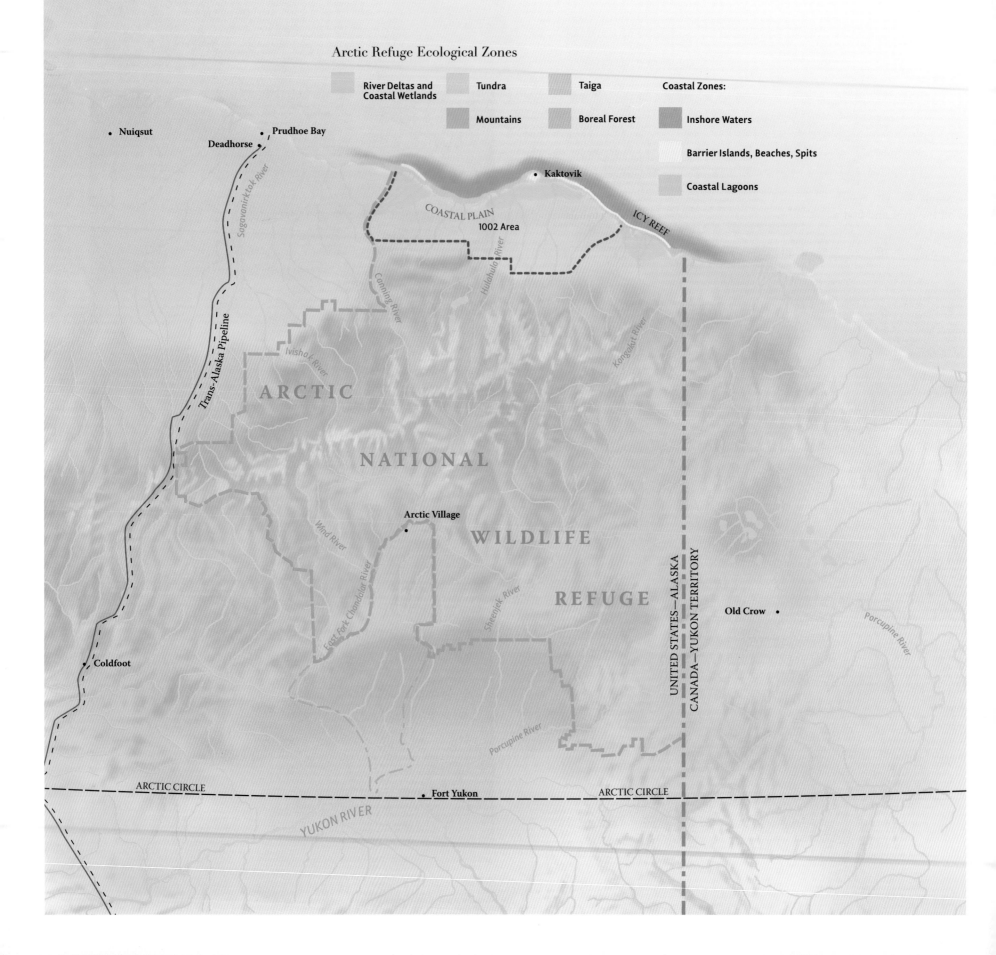

Arctic Refuge Ecological Zones

River Deltas and Coastal Wetlands

Tundra

Taiga

Mountains

Boreal Forest

Coastal Zones:

Inshore Waters

Barrier Islands, Beaches, Spits

Coastal Lagoons

Nuiqsut

Prudhoe Bay

Deadhorse

Kaktovik

Sagavanirktok River

COASTAL PLAIN

1002 Area

ICY REEF

Hulahula River

Canning River

Trans-Alaska Pipeline

Ivishak River

Kongakut River

ARCTIC

NATIONAL

Wind River

Arctic Village

WILDLIFE

East Fork Chandalar River

Sheenjek River

REFUGE

Old Crow

Porcupine River

Coldfoot

UNITED STATES—ALASKA

CANADA—YUKON TERRITORY

Porcupine River

ARCTIC CIRCLE

Fort Yukon

ARCTIC CIRCLE

YUKON RIVER

We clear another nameless mountain pass, and suddenly the Canning River is below. With no apparent landing strip in sight, Kirk banks the Cessna between steep, austere mountains, setting up for a landing in the narrow valley. What looks like a footpath through the gravel and willows is, in fact, Kirk's intended runway. Moments later we bounce down a rutted track that couldn't have been 700 feet long.

Unloading is a no-nonsense exercise. We say our good-byes and then Kirk is off, circling once to eye us a last time. We'd arranged for him to pick us up about seventy river miles and nineteen days downriver at a gravel strip, which we marked with GPS coordinates.

As the plane becomes a speck in the distance, rain starts to fall, and our pile of gear suddenly begins to look small. We move our belongings through the willows and the rain to a camping spot a few hundred yards from the strip and set up camp.

We spend two nights here—where nighttime is a daylight event—assembling our canoe, unpacking and repacking gear to find the right fit, and getting our first taste of refuge birds, mammals, and landscapes. A rafting group (two guides and a family of six from Florida) arrives by bush plane; they unload and go ahead of us down the river.

Birds around the landing strip camp are mostly passerines—White-crowned Sparrows, American Tree Sparrows, American Robins, Common Ravens, Northern Shrikes, Gray Jays, Common Redpolls. A few others are those associated with the river: Mew Gulls, Semipalmated Plovers, and Spotted Sandpipers. While hardly the species of Arctic birding dreams, these birds are a comforting mix of the familiar in a land where life clings tenuously, and tenaciously.

■ ■ ■

JULY 1. Marcia has never run white water in a canoe; I've run a lot of quick rivers, but never in a canoe with 500 pounds of gear. This is learning in the frying pan for both of us. Maneuvering and navigating the shallow channels proves to be strenuous in the fast waters of the upper Canning. If Marcia was fearful of the speeding, snaking river, she didn't show it, perhaps because she was so busy snapping the canoe bow right and then left under my urgent calls from the stern.

■ ■ ■

The first few miles are bump-and-grind canoeing. We often line or drag the canoe. The braided channels require constant attention. The scenery sweeps past, sometimes with nary a glance from us. At other times we steal peeks from the racing canoe at a Wandering Tattler we flush bank side, at Mew Gulls calling in alarm overhead. We opt not to stop and look for their nests. Perhaps the highlight of the day (other than the successful navigation of this speedy little river) is when Marcia spots a foraging dipper just after we'd gone aground in a riffle. The dipper walks a shallow bit of river, peering underwater and pecking the bottom. Water beads and rolls from its back, looking like drops of falling quicksilver; at no time does the bird appear wet. The dipper flies to a riverside cliff, landing under a small overhang. The food-begging calls of baby dippers, a high, whistling refrain, come from a grapefruit-size moss nest tucked back in a crack in the wall perhaps ten feet above the river. Two adults feed the young. One parent leaves the nest

Calf and cow moose tracks

Baird's Sandpiper

carrying a fecal sac; the other flies to a puddle and splash-lands.

We camp a short distance downriver from the dipper's nest. Birds on this stretch of the Canning River are sparse. Redpolls, robins, White-crowned Sparrows, and American Tree Sparrows frequent the willows. We have yet to see an eagle or a falcon. A hike up along a creek that tumbles out of the forbidding Franklin Mountains yields no new species of birds, but a large, fresh, black pile of grizzly bear dung brings me up short. This pile and two others I encounter are laced with the fibrous remains of a vegetable diet, despite the scattered sounds of Arctic ground squirrels. There are no ground squirrel fur or bones in the scat, but craters in the tundra mark where a griz has dug squirrels out of their burrows.

JULY 2. Last night was quiet, with little wind. I found myself on the edge of sleep, listening back into the willows to catch any sounds—not that a bear would make much sound. We tent only a few feet from thickets of willow that the redpolls and White-crowned Sparrows favor. Our site is just north of a dry creek bed that fingers down out of the mountains. In the fine alluvial mud at the creek's mouth, a string of sharp tracks attests to where a moose mother and calf have walked. We lounge riverside, watching occasional Arctic Terns work upriver against a backdrop of lupines on the mountain flanks.

JULY 3. Late in the day, Marcia and I ferry across the river and then hike upriver to observe the dipper nest again. On a dryas river terrace, a Baird's Sandpiper seems to be in the vicinity of a nest. From another terrace I catch a fleeting, distant view of a flushing Upland Sandpiper. To see the birds we must first see the habitat, and that means looking along the river in the dryas, grasses, and willows. The surrounding mountains are proving to be spectacular to ogle but nearly fruitless for birds. The river is where the action is.

JULY 4. We break camp and are soon engulfed in the fireworks of a thunderstorm. We get off the river and find a shallow gully to squat in while lightning strikes around us. Back on the water, a north wind conspires with the river to make canoe handling difficult. During a lull in the rain we pick a campsite on a low gravel bar, partly sheltered from a thirty-mile-an-hour wind. We hurry to set up the tent and then tumble into the vestibule to get out of clammy dry suits and into warmer clothes.

10:30 PM. Back home, the fireworks over Boston's Charles River will have ended. We lie in the tent, cozy but concerned about the rain and wind lashing our camp. The cloud ceiling has lowered and we hunker down, waiting for better weather so we can dash downstream. We wonder how the Baird's Sandpiper is faring, probably incubating four eggs or downy chicks, shaking off hypothermia.

JULY 5. Overnight, a sound like tiny bugs dancing on leaf litter should have been our first clue that the rain had turned to snow. We awake to four or five inches of snow blanketing our camp and the surrounding mountains, from what little we can see of them. We sit tight for the day, hemmed in by low clouds and high wind on a very gray stretch of river. Even the Wandering Tattlers we briefly see look gray, their eerie flight-songs drifting over the river bars. Back in the eight-foot-high willows we hear a cold recital from an American Tree Sparrow; add to that the alarm notes of a couple of robins, two American Pipits foraging insects on the gravel bar as I watch from the tent door, and a few redpolls dodging around—except for these, it's a quiet bird camp. In the night, the river

has risen to within a few feet of our hastily erected tent.

JULY 6. The Marsh Fork of the Canning River joins the Canning in early afternoon. A tattler forages on the west bank just downstream from the confluence. On the east bank an agitated Lesser Yellowlegs flies along with the canoe, and soon a second bird joins in. Both birds act as if a nest might be nearby, perhaps back in the willows. A Long-tailed Jaeger breezes past, the first we've seen on the trip.

■ ■ ■

The mountains have stepped back from the river. The valley seems to be widening as we paddle north. Dryas plateaus along the Canning offer better camping places, and we pick one near Plunge Creek, hoping to hike in the morning to balsam poplars in search of cavity-nesting Gray-headed Chickadees we had heard about on a tip. This is perhaps the rarest nesting bird one could find in the Canning drainage. As we descend in elevation on the river, we start to see trees in the sheltered ravines and draws. Poplars can grow to thirty feet tall and a foot in diameter in the Canning drainage. Feltleaf willow and green alder can grow here too, although alder is rare.

JULY 7. With today's gray skies and cold wind, Marcia and I lose all ambition to ferry across the river and hike up Plunge Creek. Instead we loll around camp, sleeping late, writing, and puttering. The lack of bird variety and other animals in the mountains has us looking downriver more and more. Sun tantalizes us from the foothills, but the mountains seem stuck in clouds. American Robins have been a constant at every campsite. At this camp, a robin ferries food to a low willow near a backwater. These are hardy robins—big, dark, and richly colored.

JULY 8. The patch of whitewash on the cliff was evident from upriver. We had studied the patch in the spotting scope, hoping to find bird movement, but we were too far away. Not until our little red canoe is barely abreast of the whitewash spot do we simultaneously see the youngster, both of us blurting out, "Gyrfalcon!" We quickly pull to the gravel bar across the river and drink in the single, nearly fledged chick as he eyes us from his eyrie some thirty feet above the river. Plumes of down still cling to his back and neck. We revel in the scene. Had the nest held a Rough-legged Hawk or Peregrine Falcon chick it would have been no less remarkable, but to any birder, the rare gyr chick makes the cliff an instantly recognizable place of Arctic magic. A colony of Cliff Swallows lends energy as they hawk mosquitoes over the river and bluff; a pair of Say's Phoebes commutes to a nest hidden fifteen feet above the Gyrfalcon's ledge. The nest of the gyr is not much more than a whitewashed ledge; no sticks denote this as an old Rough-legged Hawk's nest.

From the foot of the cliff we scrounge for leftover signs of previous Gyrfalcon meals. Under a perch twenty-five feet upriver, a single white ptarmigan wing marks a probable plucking perch.

Reluctantly we push downriver, but not before watching as a Rough-legged Hawk harries a Golden Eagle, the hawk working to gain altitude on the eagle before sweeping down in swift sorties.

■ ■ ■

We leave the mountains farther behind each day. Finding our fifth campsite proves problematic as we thread small channels in the area of Eagle Creek. The

American Pipit   *Savannah Sparrow*

flood plain of low willows and cobbles makes good campsites scarce, so we settle for a sandy break in the willows a few feet above a side channel. The sand turns out to be quite dusty, and, with a bit of wind, the sand quickly finds its way into everything. The camp has its charms, however. An alarmed Eastern Yellow Wagtail, an American Tree Sparrow, and a redpoll greet us upon landing. Nearby, tracks in the river mud show a wolf had recently shadowed a muskox adult with a calf. Having drinking water so close by is luxurious.

JULY 9. A section of the Canning looms large today. We expect the river could be thick with overflow ice or aufeis. We'd heard that a few weeks earlier, a rafting group rounded a river bend to find the channel blocked by aufeis. They'd had to lift their rafts up and out of the six- to eight-foot ice canyons— not a scene we wanted to repeat. We scout ahead from a hill and see an open channel. If the easy channel passage through the aufeis is a relief, the Rough-legged Hawks (at least two pairs, maybe three) we find nesting on riverside bluffs are a delight. One pair in particular was not wary. Marcia sprawls on a gravel bar and watches the female return to her nest. A nearby pair of Say's Phoebes rallies to harry the rough-legs.

Farther downriver, a wolf pauses to watch our approach on the river. We scramble to haul out binoculars. The wolf moves on in the wind, stopping twice to look back at us. The wildness and enormity of the Arctic Refuge come into focus with this one wind-buffeted predator on the move, wary and watchful.

JULY 10. We camp near Ignek Creek so we'll have a short hike to an exploratory oil well on state oil lease land on the west side of the Canning. After ferrying the river, we stash the canoe and change into hiking boots. Hiking north through the willows and then up through a steep gully to higher ground brings us to tundra thick with mosquitoes. Earlier in the day we had watched from across the river as seven bull muskox walked this same draw. At the head of the willow gully, a pair of Bluethroats, both carrying food, scolds us. We slog across the dry, tussocky tundra, and on the plateau I flush a male Smith's Longspur.

The drill pad is in view for most of the hike, and as we draw near, it proves to be three acres or more of cobbles and gravel dug from nearby tundra and fashioned into a working lot. Borrow pits that once held the gravel now hold water and foraging Red-necked Phalaropes. Eastern Yellow Wagtails and Savannah Sparrows panic over our presence at the pond edges. A Northern Harrier stops by to check on the excitement. Later, a Short-eared Owl hunts the edges of the manmade wetland. The setting highlights the tenuousness of oil in proximity to ponds and wetlands: The water attracts birds; if the well ever leaks, the wetlands would become a fatal magnet for birds.

The exploratory oil well, a large pipe sprouting from the ground, tapers to a swedge and is capped by a two-inch valve. Welded to the well pipe is a smaller pipe that sticks up eight or ten feet. That's where a welder had brazed an Exxon tiger and the words, "Exxon Company USA # A-1 Canning River Unit." Partly buried in the edges of the gravel pad are two fifty-five–gallon drums. We can't help but wonder about the contents of the drums and why they might be buried there. Are there others buried deeper—and more importantly, is it possible that their unknown contents are leaking? It's an unpleasant thought.

JULY 11. After our eight-hour foray to the exploratory well, we take a rest day at camp. We share this sandbar with another paddler, the only one we've seen since parting with the rafting group at the beginning of our trip. He says he's an oil geologist from Oklahoma, and he's against drilling in the refuge for oil. He's just returned from a hike up Ignek Creek where he reports having seen eight moose in the willows along the creek.

JULY 12. We're on the river by seven in the morning, but the wind soon rises and forces us to shore in the early afternoon. We set a hasty tent with no fly, and the wind roars. I watch a Golden Eagle trying to work his way along a series of low bluffs behind us, away from the river. Even he seems forced to hug the ground. Three times he lands in the relentless wind. A Peregrine Falcon whips past, riding an updraft from the bluff where we are hunkered.

JULY 13. By 2:30 AM the wind subsides. We strike camp and are on the river by six o'clock. We get in a few hours of paddling before the roaring headwind starts up again. Our first caribou of the trip—nearly fifty animals—shimmer in the distance. A few hard-won miles on the river bring more caribou. We camp

Exxon test well on state lease land near Section 1002

Yellow-billed Loon

on a twenty-five–foot bluff on the western shore overlooking a view of caribou hanging out on a remnant snowdrift on the opposite shore. Suddenly fifteen caribou are running; a wolf is hard on their heels. The caribou bolt for the river and plunge in, the largest bull leading the way. The wolf comes up empty.

We are on the coastal plain now, though it's difficult to say where the foothills ended and the plain began. Our campsite proves to be on a flight line for birds. The north wind deflected off the steep bank creates an updraft for the birds to sail along. Glaucous Gulls, Long-tailed Jaegers, and a peregrine sail past, hardly flapping, sometimes at eye level. The mosquitoes are grounded.

JULY 14. "I have a wolverine," says Marcia as she peers over the tundra through her spotting scope. I get on the distant galloping animal with my binoculars. His gait is part weasel, part bear, and he's hunting. Over the next forty-five minutes the wolverine pounces, lopes, and stares at caribou. They stare back. 'Rine, as we come to call him, takes an extended snow bath in the same bank where the caribou stand to avoid mosquitoes. 'Rine rubs his butt with an exaggerated sweep in the granular snow. He seems to be ecstatic with pleasure. "Happy birthday," says Marcia. The wolverine is her gift to me.

JULY 15. We break camp early to get on the river before the wind picks up. The rigors of paddling and pulling a heavy canoe have been taking a toll the last few days, and a quick four miles of paddling to the pullout leaves us with time to nurse our river wounds. I ice a sore heel with snow gathered from a bank. Our hands have slowly become chapped to the point of bleeding when we move our fingers.

From the high plateau at the pick-up strip we glass the river and see our first Yellow-billed Loon of the trip.

JULY 16. Had I planned for more time, I'd be tempted to push farther onto the coastal plain and the Canning River delta, where few paddlers venture and where, undoubtedly, we'd see more diversity of nesting shorebirds. Perhaps the delta will be the goal of a return trip. We while away the hot day reading and napping, camped not far from a ground squirrel colony, waiting for the drone

of Kirk's Cessna. Mosquitoes queue by the hundreds on our tent's netting. Somewhere nearby another Yellow-billed Loon is wailing.

■ ■ ■

POSTLOGUE: A birder visiting the Arctic will soon realize that the distribution of birds and mammals is lumpy. Large areas of—to human eyes—appropriate habitat can be bereft of birds or signs of mammals. Other seemingly identical areas can support a dense, exciting mix of shorebirds, jaegers, waterfowl, owls, arctic foxes, and wolves. In the Arctic Refuge this lumped density of life most often occurs in the grasses and tussocks of the coastal plain, with its perceived aesthetic monotony; in contrast, the spectacular landscape of the Brooks Range is a place of grand views but relatively few birds and mammals. We tallied forty-three species of birds on our nineteen-day river trip, and few of the sightings came from the mountains; our best bird and mammal sightings came from the foothills northward toward the coastal plain. Had we pressed farther into the plain and delta of the Canning, we likely would have added at least twenty-five species of birds to our list.

For Marcia and me, the refuge's influence was deep and continues to mold our thinking. Soon after returning from the refuge we replaced a thirty-mile-per-gallon car with a sixty-mile-per-gallon hybrid car. We tightened up our home's weather-stripping to save heating oil, and we started running the thermostat at lower temperatures in winter and wearing sweaters to compensate. We started paying attention to what could happen in the refuge.

For the average American who will never visit the Arctic Refuge, the closest he or she may come to the tundra is to sit behind a Toyota Tundra pickup in midtown traffic. Yet the habits and preferences of mainstream America have great impact on the very biological heart of the refuge's North Slope—the Section 1002 area. If the American public remains uninformed and indifferent, the refuge's coastal plain will be destroyed. It seems not too much to ask that we, a powerful, wealthy nation, spare the very last remnant of Alaskan Arctic coastal plain that is so terribly crucial to millions of nesting birds.

Photo: Marcia Wilson

MARK WILSON *brings a degree in biology and a love of natural history to his work as a wildlife photographer, photojournalist, writer, lecturer, and avid birder. His writing includes a biweekly birding column, "The Backyard Birder," and a weekly photography column, "Camera," which appeared in the* Boston Globe *for four and nine years respectively. He is a staff photographer at the* Globe. *His work has appeared in* National Geographic, National Wildlife, Canadian Wildlife, Yankee, Orion, *and many other magazines and books. He and his wife, teacher naturalist Marcia Wilson, often camp, canoe, and hike to study birds, wildlife, and ecosystems. The two run Eyes on Owls, an educational company that offers live owl programs.* ■

Spring Bird Research in the Arctic Refuge by Metta McGarvey

Stilt Sandpiper on nest

*O*ur group from Manomet Center for Conservation Sciences arrived on the Jago River on May 31, excited to begin documenting the distribution and density of breeding shorebirds throughout the coastal plain. The weather ranges from freezing fog with gale-force winds to glorious, sunny days in the fifties.

Today starts at 6:30 AM with the lovely woo-woo-woo-woo-woo of a male Pectoral Sandpiper. Shorebirds produce a spectacular symphony of breeding and territorial calls during the twenty-four–hour daylight in June. It's thirty-eight degrees and foggy. By 8:30 we've had breakfast and loaded data sheets and equipment into our daypacks, together with twenty pounds of survival gear, GPS units, field glasses, water, and food. We carry twelve-gauge shotguns for bear protection.

Four team members are transported by helicopter to conduct rapid surveys of randomly selected, forty-acre sites across this 1.5-million-acre region—110 sites in total—while I and three others rotate among eight intensively studied sites within walking distance of camp. A surprising range of habitats makes walking an adventure. Shallow bogs, with slick permafrost underneath, suck hard on our hip boots, making each step a slurping test of determination. Upland areas of tussock tundra transform walking into a fatiguing, comical wobble across a field of stubbly softballs.

Two long miles from camp I begin recording breeding-bird displays. Observing a Semipalmated Sandpiper and Stilt Sandpiper as they forage, I track each back to its nest. On past visits to this site we documented one Red-necked Phalarope nest and two Pectoral Sandpiper nests, along with the nests of two Lapland Longspurs and one Long-tailed Duck. I carefully recheck these to make sure they have not been destroyed by predators. The birds sit tight for a remarkably long time, flushing only when I'm about fifteen yards away.

Around 7:30 PM, after surveying my second site, I hike back to camp. Changing from hip boots to hiking boots and fresh socks is a welcome relief. During dinner, the floor of the tent undulates: A lemming is making its home beneath the temporary shelter. At 10:45 PM we write up data and finish with our camp chores. The mountains are stunningly clear, and in the long light of the midnight sun, birds sing like it is morning. We hear the dee-dee-dee-dee-dee-burr of a Long-billed Dowitcher; a Stilt Sandpiper calls high above, ending with the braying sound of a donkey.

Lying on camp pads nestled between tussocks, we listen. Two Red-necked Phalaropes softly coo as they forage in the pond just feet from our tent. We hear the wild calls and gentle mewing of many pairs of Pacific Loons on ponds near and far. Their powerful voices, found only in wilderness, fall on too many deaf ears. This research is how we can help them be heard, help protect this one last precious piece of undeveloped Arctic coastal wilderness and the millions of birds and animals whose lives depend on it. Long days and sore feet are a small price for the privilege of being in this place that needs more than anything for us to simply let it be. ▪

Loons and

Waterfowl

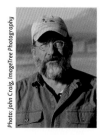

Jeff Fair *is a wildlife*

biologist with four books to

his credit, including Moose

for Kids *and* The Great American Bear. *His*

essays have appeared in Alaska Magazine, The

Christian Science Monitor, *the* Boston Globe,

Equinox, Ranger Rick, Audubon Magazine,

and Appalachia, *where he is a contributing*

editor. In 1998 he received the National Wildlife

Federation's Farrand/Strohm Writing Award,

and in 2001 he was selected for the Alaska State

Council on the Arts' first Tumblewords roster.

Overleaf ■ *Hulahula River and Okpilak River delta*

THE CANNING RIVER DELTA, ARCTIC NATIONAL WILDLIFE REFUGE
JUNE 4, 1:07 AM

All night long under the midnight sun, the Arctic sings its spring song. Floating in from somewhere behind the wind are the voices of this land: the various musics of Greater White-fronted and Canada Geese, Pacific and Red-throated Loons, and Long-tailed Ducks (we used to call them Oldsquaws), along with a few quieter fowl I cannot name. Nestled in the candlelike glow inside my yellow tent, I lie awake, listening. The temperature hovers below freezing, half the tundra remains covered in snow, the lakes are still frozen over—but these water birds, eternal optimists of the Arctic plains, are arriving 'round the clock, en masse and in voice, for their summer ventures. Off to the north I hear the excited chatter of Tundra Swans. A few hours ago, outside my tent I looked up and watched seven of them materialize out of the mist: elegant, slow-winged creatures pure as snow, passing closely above with the grace of angels.

■ ■ ■

Bowing into the morning fog on a raw northeast wind, I make my way to the cook tent to build a mug of boreal coffee. Six of us have established a temporary research camp here on the northern fringe of the delta, in the very northwestern corner of the refuge. I've joined the others as a volunteer biologist for a study of the nesting success of the local birdlife.

We arrived by bush plane over the past two days, as weather allowed, and set up our bivouac: six identical sleeping tents crowd together like a clutch of eggs, and fifty yards off stands a cooking tent and a warming tent with a wood stove. Farther yet our tiny, makeshift latrine enjoys a holy and priceless view. The tents are staked against the arctic wind with foot-long pieces of rebar hammered into the frozen ground. Yesterday we used ice chisels and sledges to pound larger holes to erect two separate three-wire bear fences, one around our sleeping quarters and one around the food tents. There are a few griz about, and we hope to see them, but they are not welcome inside. The fences are electrified by solar panels—powered by the sun like the living tundra itself.

*Abandon, as in love or sleep, holds
the ancient faith: what we need is here.*

"The Wild Geese," from *The Selected Poems of Wendell Berry*

Around us stretches the vast Arctic prairie, now a mosaic of white snow and golden brown cottongrass and sedges. When the ocean fog lifts (camp is only two miles from the shore of the Beaufort Sea), we can see thirty miles south to the Sadlerochits, last mountains before the North Pole, and beyond them to the massive Brooks Range, blue and infinite in the distance.

Out of the fog and that infinity, the feathered tribe continues to arrive. More Tundra Swans wing in from their winter waters on the Chesapeake Bay; White-fronted geese appear, with their high-pitched laughter, up from the Texas coast. The loons have come all the way from the Yellow Sea off China. We see two long lines of Black Brant—a subspecies of Brant—fifty or more in each, flying eastward, low over the whitened tundra along the coast, nearing the end of their jaunt from Mexico. Must be something about this place, something attractive and valuable that draws them here. Otherwise, why would so many species come from so many distant places for the most important function of life—reproduction? And I don't mean only water birds. Arctic Terns and many of the shorebirds return here from even more distant places. Caribou and polar bears choose to give birth here. What some have blindly called a barren wasteland appears to me more like a coral reef of the north, a huge sponge of productivity.

Ten Snow Geese, then twenty more, fly across, white as alabaster under a cerulean blue sky. Pintails, Common Eiders, and King Eiders arc overhead in pairs and small groups. The commons are more likely to move out to the coastal barrier islands to breed. A drake King Eider flies close by at eye level. His body is black and white, but his head is the marvel: red bill, orange forehead, green cheek, blue crown and nape—nearly the full spectrum from the neck forward. The Harlequin Ducks are nearly as audacious, but we won't see them here. They nest up in the mountains, where they walk underwater along the stream bottoms, foraging into the current in the fashion that the water ouzel made famous.

Of all the birds that nest in the refuge, I consider the Pacific Loon the most elegant. With its velvet gray hood, splendid black-and-white collar and cape, and polished poise on the water, it embodies a reserved handsomeness, dignity,

and grace. I say this without bias, although my work has focused on loons for nearly three decades. In truth, I haven't studied Pacific and Red-throated Loons much at all and still have a difficult time separating their voices.

Today we make our first formal visit to two of the twenty research plots established three years ago when the study began. My compatriots take a primary, focused interest in the shorebirds, our most numerous clients on the swaths of tundra. I'm keeping an eye out for loons and waterfowl—the larger feathered spirits. There's something about how a swan can raise its cygnets from eggs to fifteen pounds over a short Arctic summer by eating cold vegetables that seems magic to me. The local Inupiat still hunt these creatures, and their knowledge of them is based upon the oldest research ever undertaken in these parts: the science of survival.

· · ·

Swans float about like icebergs on the river in front of camp. A single Red-throated Loon rockets downriver. One minute later: cacophony at the river bend. She's found some friends—or maybe antagonists. It's hard to tell, given the caterwauling. Either way, it resounds with excitement.

As my colleagues pointed out, the racket these two species make can hardly be called a song at all. And by strict definition they are correct. Any ornithological text or field guide will tell you that neither loons nor waterfowl sing songs; they utter *calls*. In the absolute scientific sense, this is true. Problem is, I'm not an absolute scientist; romantic biologist might be a better description. I cherish these voices because they symbolize the north lands that I love. And if, as the bioacousticians suggest, these voices are tuned to carry through misty winds and above the white sound of driven waters, then they are tuned by the landscape—they are voices of the land, much as their very bodies are built of and powered by local stickleback and blackfish. Even the Red-throated Loon's cry, compared by some to the sound of a cat in despair, rings eerily melodic if you happen to carry an affinity for loons as I do. To my ear all these voices, in their innocent melancholy and exuberance, reach to that place where laughter

and tears meld, and life celebrates itself upon the land. It is music to me.

The wind whips up again in the evening, rattling and wrestling with the tents, another night of wild percussion drummed into our delicate human spirits. The wind, too, is a voice of the land—that same wind that lifts the wings of Tundra Swans and carries the yodels of loons.

■ ■ ■

Every day we walk the plots. Lapland Longspurs and a few sandpipers have already begun nesting in tiny alcoves in the sun-warmed and hay-scented tundra. The snowfields are disappearing by the acre despite the biting cold of the wind. Ice water collects in the polygons, fills the ponds, and seeps in slow, cold currents through the grasses and sedges into the river and down toward the sea. On average, only seven inches of precipitation fall here each year, but it's hard to think of this place as a "polar desert" when we're marching through water up to our knees. Unable to soak very deeply into the soil due to the solid barrier of permafrost, the snowmelt remains on the surface, available to wildlife and irrigating the grasses and sedges. Often we wade across ponds filled with a layer of water above ankle-deep muck, our soles treading upon the concrete hardpan of ice—the permafrost.

Purple saxifrage, first of the Arctic blooms, flowers around us from its low cushions on the drier soils. East of camp I found a broad scatter of swan feathers, a few bone fragments. Over by the river we stumbled onto the skull and rib cage of an arctic fox. A few miles to the north lies the entire skeleton of a muskox, its flesh eaten and the long bones gnawed apart. Here and there on the tundra we find the shells of Long-tailed Duck eggs, the antlers and ribs of caribou. We watch for the droppings of foxes and wolves, deposited on the peat mounds and often twisted with the hair of lemmings and occasionally caribou, sometimes containing the tips of feather shafts. There's a grizzly track frozen into last year's mud near my tent. On the riverbank we see many tracks—all sizes and makes of waterfowl—along with those of fox and weasel, and now and then a burst of feathers. All the chapters of life here lie open to the sky. Every walk is a treasure hunt.

■ ■ ■

Cold again; windy as usual. My crew finds the first Canada Goose nest today near study plot 4B: four eggs nestled in gray down upon a grassy bowl on a small island. The Tundra Swans, first of the waterfowl to nest, are incubating too, down on the lower delta.

Loons of both species, often singly, fly overhead almost constantly now, in different directions, reconnoitering the melt waters, one might assume. Loons are, of course, not waterfowl at all. According to current theory, they are more closely related to penguins and frigatebirds. Adapted to diving, they navigate poorly on land and require stretches of open water for take-offs and landings. Because of this, they will be among the last to alight upon the lakes as they thaw.

More and more waterfowl arrive. Red-breasted Mergansers have appeared, as well as a pair of Northern Shovelers. Someone has seen a pair of Spectacled Eiders, a threatened species listed formally under the Endangered Species Act

and a rare nester here. Most of the United States Arctic population nests farther west, where oil leases are likely to be developed. But this was a pair, male and female, and they are known to prefer river deltas, so we are hopeful.

The Long-tailed Ducks would make an interesting study. Tens of thousands of them molt and gather into large groups to stage on the lagoons behind the barrier islands before fall migration. We see them floating, almost always in pairs, on the coldest-looking little ponds among chunks of ice. Common breeders on the coastal plain, they are unusual in two ways. Unlike the other waterfowl, Long-tailed Ducks utter sentence-long calls and molt continually in a sequence of phases from spring through fall, rendering a long series of ephemeral appearances far too numerous and variable to be represented in any field guide. Though ornately beautiful in earthen tones, for half the year it is impossible to match their color patterns with any page in a field guide.

Off the corner of plot 4A I spot a Peregrine Falcon sitting dark and quiet upon a low peat mound, waiting patiently. There's a reason the Peregrine was once called a "duck hawk," but this hunter is more likely watching for the rustle of a sandpiper or a nice, warm lemming. (There are a lot of lemmings about this year, which might take some of the predation pressure off of the birdlife.) We honor the peregrine's presence by pausing our survey so as not to scare up any study birds, duck or Dunlin, for its dinner. I carry no prejudice against predators, myself. After all, I belong to that league, and so does the cute little arctic fox, and the loon. We're all part of the balance.

The wind howls, coating my spectacles with droplets of fog, burning color into the skin of my cheeks. A harsh land? Some would say so. Who could deny it? But it is this very harshness that illuminates by contrast the abundant and exuberant life here—song and sex and celebration, bloom and productivity. The harshness of winter here drastically reduces the numbers of predators. And the

Opposite ■ Snow Geese over the coastal plain, Brooks Range in the background / Canada Goose

Hawks, Eagles,

and Falcons

Shorebirds

The restlessness of shorebirds, their kinship with
of their voices down the long coastlines of the
wild creatures. I think of them as birds

STEPHEN BROWN *is the director of the Shorebird Conservation Research Program at Manomet Center for Conservation Sciences and has studied shorebirds and their wetland habitats for twenty years. He received his doctorate from Cornell University, where he studied restoration of wetland bird habitats. Brown is the lead author of "The United States Shorebird Conservation Plan" as well as more than twenty peer-reviewed articles on shorebirds and wetland management. He conducts field studies on the distribution and abundance of shorebirds in the Arctic National Wildlife Refuge and collaborates on other shorebird research and conservation projects throughout the country.*

Overleaf ■ Tundra in spring

In early August, the fleeting Arctic summer begins to wane, and the wildlife of the Arctic Refuge coastal plain starts to prepare for another long winter. As the sun begins to set briefly each night for the first time in months, one of the most remarkable feats of migration in the animal world starts to unfold. Many of the adult shorebirds that flew north to breed only a few months earlier have already left their recently hatched young and begun their long journeys south. The juvenile shorebirds, hatched only weeks before on the Arctic tundra, are preparing to follow. They have only recently lost the small tufts of downy feathers they wore upon emerging from their eggs and grown their first full set of flight feathers. After a few short weeks of instruction by their parents in such vital activities as hiding from predators, they must face the world on their own.

These fledglings will now migrate across two continents, without a map or any help from their parents, to a place they have never seen. They will make their way across thousands of miles of unknown landscapes following only their instincts. Remarkably, each generation somehow finds the far-flung wintering grounds unique to their species, ranging from the southern coast of the United States to the South Pacific to the farthest southern tip of South America. They are ambassadors from the Arctic to the rest of the world, and they carry with them clues about the health of the world's ecosystems. Those that manage to survive the arduous migrations will help produce the future generations of Arctic wings, carrying on the cycle of endless movement that has graced the tundra for millennia.

■ ■ ■

The term *shorebird* is applied to a large group of birds that includes the familiar sandpipers and plovers but also includes oystercatchers, avocets, stilts, and jacanas. Many other common birds of the shoreline, such as gulls and terns, are classified in other bird families. There are 222 kinds of shorebirds worldwide; 71 occur regularly in North America, and shorebirds are found in many different habitats throughout the continent. Shorebirds often share similar

the distance and swift seasons, the wistful signal world make them, for me, the most affecting of of the wind, as "wind birds."

Peter Matthiessen, *The Wind Birds*

characteristics such as relatively long bills for probing in wet mud and sand, long legs for standing in water or mud, and long pointed wings for fast flight over long distances.

Most people know shorebirds as demure creatures that follow the coastlines and freshwater edges of the world, quietly going about their business of finding something to eat. Like other birds that fall silent in winter, shorebirds do not vocalize much during migration or on their wintering grounds. But their reputation of silence is misleading, an accident of geography that recalls the famous line about a tree falling in the forest: Shorebirds are little known for their singing because most of us aren't there to hear them when they sing. When they arrive on their Arctic breeding grounds in late May, they burst into song, vividly advertising for mates and staking out their territories. Few bird sounds are as lovely and haunting as the song of a Stilt Sandpiper flying high above its territory while the midnight sun glances off the tundra.

RESTLESS MIGRANTS

Shorebirds complete some of the longest-distance migrations of all animals. Many of the most highly migratory shorebirds use a "long-hop" strategy, with some sections of their journeys completed in long, nonstop flights. Bar-tailed Godwits fly more than 7000 miles from Alaska across the Pacific Ocean to New Zealand without stopping for food, rest, or water. Other species may cover long migration journeys in a series of short flights. Some of the relatively short- and moderate-distance migrants have nonstop flight segments that vary from a few hundred miles to thousands of miles.

Shorebird migration patterns are diverse. Although each species is different, there are three general patterns in North America. Some migration routes connect Alaska with Pacific islands and continents as distant as Australia. Other routes follow the Pacific Coast and western mountain cordilleras of North and South America. Still others connect the Arctic breeding grounds with the Caribbean Basin and northeastern South America, with some of these

passing through central regions of the Lower 48 states and others concentrated in Atlantic coastal regions. Many of the shorebirds that nest in the Arctic Refuge spend the rest of the year in sites all across North America, South America, and Australasia.

■ ■ ■

Why would a Semipalmated Sandpiper, which weighs about as much as a double-A battery, go to all the trouble of flying from South America to the Arctic

Bar-tailed Godwit

SHOREBIRD BREEDING DISTRIBUTION IN THE ARCTIC NATIONAL WILDLIFE REFUGE

A total of twenty-six shorebird species regularly use the Arctic National Wildlife Refuge during some part of their life cycle, and nine more (Killdeer, Eurasian Dotterel, Black-tailed Godwit, Hudsonian Godwit, Red Knot, Red-necked Stint, Sharp-tailed Sandpiper, Ruff, and Wilson's Phalarope) have been recorded as migrants or visitors. Twenty-three species are known to breed in the refuge, and some breed both on the coastal plain and to the south. Three more species—Solitary Sandpiper, Bar-tailed Godwit, and Western Sandpiper—may breed in the Arctic Refuge, but nesting has not been confirmed.

SHOREBIRDS THAT BREED ON THE ARCTIC REFUGE COASTAL PLAIN

Black-bellied Plover
American Golden-Plover
Semipalmated Plover
Wandering Tattler
Spotted Sandpiper
Upland Sandpiper
Whimbrel
Ruddy Turnstone
Sanderling
Semipalmated Sandpiper
White-rumped Sandpiper
Baird's Sandpiper
Pectoral Sandpiper
Dunlin
Stilt Sandpiper
Buff-breasted Sandpiper
Long-billed Dowitcher
Red-necked Phalarope
Red Phalarope

SHOREBIRDS THAT BREED SOUTH OF THE COASTAL PLAIN

American Golden-Plover
Semipalmated Plover
Lesser Yellowlegs
Wandering Tattler
Spotted Sandpiper
Upland Sandpiper
Whimbrel
Surfbird
Least Sandpiper
Baird's Sandpiper
Wilson's Snipe
Red-necked Phalarope

to reproduce—and then leave the Arctic for the long flight back to its wintering ground? Surprisingly, avoiding the harsh cold of the Arctic winter is probably not the most important reason to migrate south; in fact, several species of birds do manage to overwinter in the refuge. Instead, finding adequate food is probably the most important cause for the round-trip flight. Shorebirds follow the sun, living in the Arctic during the long northern summer days, and traveling south for the northern hemisphere's winter to places where the southern summer is in full swing. This strategy provides two important advantages simultaneously. First, it gives the birds access to the seasonal blooms of invertebrate life that accompany spring and summer in each hemisphere. Second, it gives them long days during which to forage. This is especially important for birds that forage along the coast, where the tides already limit their access to prime feeding areas.

The American Golden-Plover is a favorite among birders for its striking plumage of jet black face and underparts, bold white stripe above the black, and delicately flecked golden and brown upper parts. These birds are a good example of the epic migrations shorebirds undertake and are famous for an unusual twist in their pattern: They pass through North America's interior wet prairies as they head north in the spring but take a different route on the way south in the fall, as though wanting to see more of the countryside than an average shorebird (see map later in this chapter).

After wintering primarily on grasslands and inland wetlands of Argentina, Chile, Paraguay, Uruguay, and southern Bolivia, American Golden-Plovers travel north through the Amazonian regions of South America to arrive on the U.S. gulf coastal plain in March and April. They continue into the North American heartland, where they are commonly seen on farmed fields, before moving on to their Arctic breeding grounds in May to June. But most individuals opt for a fall migration route that is far to the east, taking advantage of summer fruit production along the coast before launching an astonishing 2500-mile nonstop flight over water to South America.

As though not quite up for this extreme migratory challenge, or perhaps just doing their best at finding their way for the first time, many juveniles repeat their parents' spring route in reverse during the fall, taking shorter trips between inland stopover sites on their way south. Only in later years will they somehow learn about the possibility of using the ocean route to fly south. Unfortunately, this species is declining at alarming rates along the eastern coastline of the United States during fall migration. If these declines continue, the species may be in serious jeopardy.

▪ ▪ ▪

So what does it take for a shorebird to succeed at a massive nonstop migration? Fat. While humans often avoid fattening foods and carefully watch their weight, a shorebird getting ready for migration seeks out fats and consumes them at remarkable rates that completely belie the phrase, "to eat like a bird." To imagine eating enough to double your weight in only a month, consider this: An average human male weighing 160 pounds would be required to consume about 560,000 extra calories that month—on top of a normal diet. This is about the equivalent of eating 1600 cheeseburgers—that's 53 every day for a month! If our man was a vegetarian, he would need to eat 1244 bean burritos laden with cheese and sour cream, or 41 each day all month. In either case, he'd need a lot of antacid.

Even more remarkable is that a fat shorebird can get airborne and fly nonstop for days, consuming all of those fat reserves along the way. A human would have a hard time moving at all, much less walking nonstop to South America. At an average speed of about three miles an hour, walking eight hours a day, our imaginary human migrant would take over a year to make the same trip many shorebirds accomplish in just a few days. In fact, it would take more than a day to travel the distance in a jet airliner, and we would be tired on arrival without having taken a single step. But for shorebirds these marathon flights are commonplace, their link between global habitats in their search for food en route to and from their breeding grounds.

MIXING IT UP ON THE BREEDING GROUNDS

When the first ornithologists watched nesting birds, they assumed there generally were one male and one female per nest, and they sometimes exhorted people to follow these paragons of monogamous virtue—that is, until they started actually marking birds so they could tell them apart and keep track of which ones were doing what. As it turns out, Arctic shorebirds participate in just about every kind of mating strategy one can imagine. While we tend to apply our human values to other creatures, in the struggle for survival in the wild, the most effective mating strategy often is not monogamy.

Some shorebirds use an unusual mating strategy called polyandry, in which more than one male mates with a single female. Particularly enterprising females of some species, including both the Red and Red-necked Phalaropes common in the Arctic Refuge, sometimes finish laying one nest with one male and then move on to start another family with another willing male. Each male is then relegated to raising the chicks alone. On first appearance, it might seem as if the females have it easy, but all this egg laying is a Herculean task in itself. The females engage in the costly behavior of dual nesting only occasionally, perhaps when food is unusually abundant. In producing two complete clutches of four eggs, a female Red-necked Phalarope will have laid about 1.8 ounces of egg in a matter of days—which doesn't seem like much, except that she herself weighs only about 1.2 ounces. Imagine an average human mother of 140 pounds giving birth to nineteen children at perhaps 11 pounds each, and collectively weighing half again as much as the mother, and you'll have some idea of how taxing this might be!

For some shorebirds, such as the Pectoral Sandpiper, males who can manage it occasionally attract multiple females in a mating strategy called polygyny. For ornithologists, polygyny makes counting birds in the field very challenging because it is tough to tell whether a particular male is associated with one or many females. A firm number of pairs is difficult to determine, and so breeding male territories generally are used as an index of population size. Apparently, polygyny is a function either of quality of a territory or female choice. When a particularly robust male has the strength to maintain a high-quality territory with enough space and food for two females, or otherwise proves attractive due to his great condition, two or more females may decide he's the best choice to father their young. Subsequently, each female lays a nest in his territory rather than that of another nearby male. It makes for a lot of work for the male, because he must constantly fight off other males who try to sneak into his territory and mate with his females. In many bird species, multiple paternity has been determined through genetic analysis, implying that males have a hard time successfully defending territories. But the aggravation apparently is worth the effort, measured in the number of chicks that survive to reproduce and carry on their paternal lineage.

Shorebird chicks have a short childhood. Within a day of hatching, most are able to walk and search for their own food. In the case of Red-necked Phalaropes, the males help chicks stay warm by brooding them, but only for about the first week of life, until their newly grown feathers can maintain their proper temperature. Further parental assistance may include introducing them to foraging areas and perhaps giving a guided tour to the nearby staging areas along the coast, where phalaropes concentrate at the end of the summer. After that, the young chicks are on their own.

HABITAT AND CONSERVATION

Shorebirds, like all other wildlife, need appropriate habitats in which to live: during breeding, during the non-breeding season, and along migration routes. This makes conservation especially challenging, because to ensure the health of their populations, we must protect not only their breeding grounds in the Arctic Refuge but also a great many other key sites that they use throughout the year.

Some species rely heavily upon a small number of strategic migration

American Golden-Plover   *Red Phalarope*

stopover sites to successfully complete their migration to and from the Arctic, and because of this a large percentage of a population might be present at a single site at the same time. For example, most of the Red-necked Phalaropes that hatch each year in the Arctic Refuge converge in August along the narrow Arctic coastline. Here, coastal lagoons and intertidal mudflats provide critical habitat as the young birds gain energy stores for their epic migrations to southern oceans. Similarly, between 50 and 80 percent of Red Knots, which are sometimes seen as migrants along the Arctic Refuge coast, stage at Delaware Bay, between Delaware and New Jersey, during their northward movement in spring. And the majority of Buff-breasted Sandpipers, a rare species that nests on the Arctic Refuge coastal plain, were recorded during migration at only ten sites across the United States.

The health of these traditional sites is critical, and disruption at any of the essential sites along the migration corridors could have catastrophic results. Recognition of this special aspect of shorebird biology and the need to devise novel conservation strategies were the major factors that led to the creation of the Western Hemisphere Shorebird Reserve Network, which aims to protect critical shorebird sites in both North and South America.

Seasonal wetlands, which may be available only once every several years, are another key shorebird habitat. These pothole wetlands may hold water one year and be dry the next, which causes great variance in the numbers of shorebirds using these wetlands in any particular year. The value of habitat for migrating shorebirds in areas such as the Prairie Pothole region of the upper Midwest or the Playa Lakes region of the southern U.S. prairies tends to be underestimated since these wetlands typically are small and dispersed, and the numbers of birds using any particular site may be few. But when a complex of

Pectoral Sandpiper

wetlands is considered as a whole, these ephemeral habitats are critical to the survival of many shorebirds that breed in the Arctic Refuge and then travel widely throughout the rest of the hemisphere.

Populations of almost all kinds of shorebirds have been affected by loss of essential habitats. Some species have suffered severe habitat loss in both migration and wintering areas. In general, breeding habitat loss has been minimal for boreal and Arctic-breeding shorebirds, but there is growing concern that global warming may change this. The latitude at which shrubs can grow and thrive has been expanding northward due to warmer conditions caused by global climate change, and it is likely that in the coming decades, substantial breeding habitat loss may occur across the North Slope.

Loss of migration habitat already has been extensive for many species. Development and human recreational activities along the coasts have grown enormously since European settlement, reducing intertidal habitats and the diversity and abundance of food eaten by foraging shorebirds. And equally important, coastal development has resulted in the usurping of resting areas used by shorebirds when mudflats and shallow feeding grounds are inundated at high tide. For shorebirds, migration stopover sites play a vital role in their effort to build the reserves they need to fuel the next leg of migration. If they are unsuccessful in gaining the necessary fat, shorebirds don't make it to the next stop, and consequently adult survival rates decline. Because the majority of Arctic breeding shorebirds migrate southward throughout the United States during July to September, they directly compete with humans for coastal space during the peak of summer outdoor recreation season.

THE RACE TO SAVE THE SHOREBIRDS

Each wildlife species attempts to reproduce and replenish its numbers, but its population tends to be limited by some critical factor. For shorebirds, perhaps not enough young hatch each year; many young birds don't survive; adult birds die from contaminants; or they can't return to the breeding grounds because food supplies along the way are too low. But because of the variety of challenges that these birds face, and the difficulty of measuring how important each factor is, we don't yet have a solid grasp of the specific causes for most of the declines that have been observed in shorebird populations. This lack of knowledge means that we must take a precautionary approach and work to protect all of the areas critical to shorebirds, while at the same time making efforts to learn more about the problems they face. A new effort called the Shorebird Research Group of the Americas was recently formed to coordinate hemispheric work on these questions for the species suffering the greatest declines. We hope that the critical information will come in time to help reverse the downward trends.

The oil development proposed for the Arctic Refuge must be weighed in this context, as it represents another potentially large risk for many species that already are in trouble. Direct effects of oil drilling in the refuge include loss of nesting habitat due to construction on the breeding grounds and

American Golden-Plovers:
Key Migration Routes and Breeding and Wintering Ranges

Breeding Area   Principal Wintering Areas

→ Autumn Migration   → Spring Migration

Source: M. Boughman, Reference Atlas to the Birds of North America. National Geographic Society, 2003.

SHOREBIRD NESTING HABITAT IN THE ARCTIC NATIONAL WILDLIFE REFUGE

WETLAND

MIXED TUNDRA

FOOTHILL UPLANDS

ROCKY RIVERBED

BOG

In their selection of places to raise their young, shorebirds have very wide-ranging tastes. Some species nest only in wetland areas where marshes, teeming with invertebrates, are separated by small ridges that offer a drier area perfect for concealing a nest. In the Arctic Refuge, Pectoral Sandpipers, Semipalmated Sandpipers, and the phalaropes are typical of this group.

Left: Pectoral Sandpiper nest; far left: Pectoral Sandpiper

American Golden-Plover nests typically are found on drier ridges in areas with marshy wetlands nearby.

Left: American Golden-Plover nest; far left: American Golden-Plover

Other species prefer nest sites with a view and opt for upland areas in the foothills or the Brooks Range. Typical breeders in the Brooks Range include Upland and Baird's Sandpipers. Surfbirds prefer the bare, high alpine areas found here.

Left: Baird's Sandpiper

Some shorebirds prefer rocky Arctic riverbeds for nesting sites. They include Semipalmated Plovers and Ruddy Turnstones.

Left: Semipalmated Plover

And some shorebirds nest around bogs in the forested south slope of the Arctic Refuge, such as Solitary, Spotted, and Least Sandpipers; Lesser Yellowlegs; and Wilson's Snipe.

Left: Lesser Yellowlegs

Caribou herd migrates across tundra, habitat used by shorebirds to nest earlier in the season

changes in vegetation from seismic exploration activities. Some indirect effects include oil-spill contamination, which inevitably accompanies oil development; changes in drainage patterns around roads, which can adversely affect habitats; and potential increases in predation rates on shorebird nests by those predators that are drawn to human habitation and refuse. How much impact there might be from these various factors is difficult to predict, but we do know that further declines in already-diminished populations will only make matters worse.

No one knows for certain where oil might be found under the Arctic Refuge coastal plain, but it is likely that the pattern of oil distribution outside the refuge, which is clustered along the coast, may continue under the refuge as well. If oil development is allowed in the refuge, it would certainly take place within the small coastal plain area. Our research in the Arctic Refuge has shown that the coastal plain hosts enough shorebirds to qualify as a Site of International Importance under the Western Hemisphere Shorebird Reserve Network and

as a Wetland of International Importance under the Ramsar Convention on Wetlands. In addition, our work has shown that the coastal wetlands support the greatest numbers and species diversity of Arctic shorebirds—critical habitat needed to ensure that enough young shorebirds hatch each year to replace the adults lost to the risks of long migrations.

Protecting key breeding areas like the Arctic Refuge coastal plain is an essential step toward preserving the populations of these remarkable migrants, who travel to and depend on so many different places scattered throughout the Western Hemisphere to support their long-distance lifestyle. Their travels as ambassadors from the Arctic make clear the connectedness of ecosystems throughout the hemisphere. Considering their death-defying migrations and the long odds they face along the way, the spectacle of shorebird migration is perfectly humbling. Protecting them will require all our diligence and ingenuity. In this process, if shorebird migrations have a lesson to teach us, it might simply be to cast fear and doubt aside, and attempt the seemingly impossible. ∎

Gulls, Terns,

and Jaegers

Owls

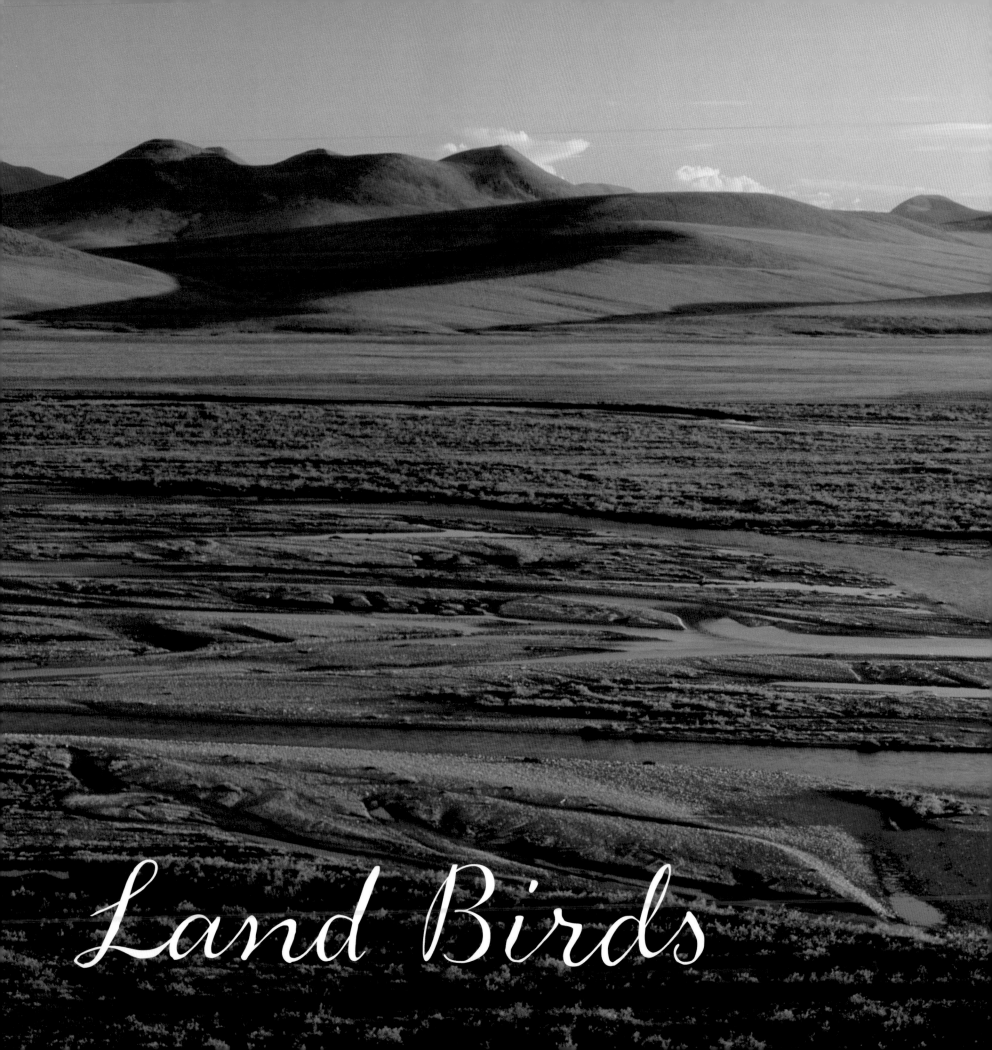

Land Birds

Winter Birds

FRANK KEIM *is a retired*

high school teacher who

taught for twenty-one years

in four Yupik villages in the Lower Yukon School

District in Southwest Alaska, at the mouth of

the Yukon River. He lived for many years in

Latin America, where he was a Peace Corps

Volunteer and an anthropology instructor

at the University of Cuenca. Keim is on the

Alaska State Board of Trustees of the National

Audubon Society and regularly contributes

articles to local and regional publications. He

is a nature poet and wood-carver. He learned

his love of birds and walking from his father

when he was very young, and he hopes his own

children and grandchildren will learn the same

from him.

Overleaf ■ *Okpilak River valley*

The strangest thing happened to me before I started writing this essay. I was on a week-long kayak trip in Prince William Sound when, one cool, windy night, I had a dream about the winter birds of the Arctic National Wildlife Refuge. I warn you, it was a bizarre dream. Let me try to remember.

All the birds that reside in the Arctic Refuge during the winter were gathered around a campfire in the nocturnal dark of the boreal forest. There was deep snow on the ground, and a wall of black-green spruce surrounded this confraternity of birds. Both predators and prey were present, but they all seemed to be getting along; in fact, they were downright sociable with one another. The yellow flames of the fire flickered off their feathers and beaked faces, and not a scowl or a smirk or a suspicious glint could be seen in any of their eyes.

Glancing around the fire, I counted twenty-six species: Starting with Common Raven, who seemed to be the ringleader, there was his cousin, Gray Jay; then American Dipper, Boreal Chickadee, and her two cousins, Black-capped and Gray-headed Chickadees. Next to them were five of the grouse family: Rock and Willow Ptarmigan, and Spruce, Sharp-tailed, and Ruffed Grouse. In a quiet huddle were four woodpeckers: American Three-toed, Downy, Hairy, and Black-backed. Then there were five owls deep in serious conversation: Boreal Owl, Northern Hawk Owl, Snowy Owl, Great Gray Owl, and Great Horned Owl. Gyrfalcon was next, chatting with his neighbor, Northern Goshawk. Completing the circle were the four colorful winter finches: White-winged Crossbill, Pine Grosbeak, and Hoary and Common Redpolls. The last three were glancing at their neighbor, Common Raven, and gesturing at their suitcases. They were getting ready to move to Fairbanks if the temperatures plummeted any lower.

It was a motley group, to be sure, but they were well adapted for this harsh Arctic environment in ways that their insect-eating cousins were not. Raven began to speak about a story that was being written about them, one that told readers why they stayed in the Arctic Refuge during winter while their cousins

Everyone is born with a bird in his heart.

Frank M. Chapman

flew south to warmer climates. I listened and heard words from the other side of the fire ask, "But what makes us winter birds, anyway?" Then suddenly my dream ended in a noisy crash.

What had happened, I wondered? Had a tree fallen, or had a bear come into camp? I peered out of my tent and saw an overturned cooking pot next to a Gray Jay. I rubbed my eyes and asked myself, "Am I still dreaming?"

I wished I were, because I wanted to hear what the birds had to say about what constituted a winter bird. I tried going back to sleep to continue the dream, but finally I gave up, deciding in any case that this would be a good place to begin my story.

■ ■ ■

In the context of the Arctic National Wildlife Refuge, a winter bird is any species that remains within the boundaries of the refuge in significant numbers for twelve months of the year. During some frigid winters there may be exceptions, such as the three species of finch in my dream that sometimes move a little farther south at this time. With the present warmer trends in weather, these finches undoubtedly will begin to stay year round in the southern corner of the refuge.

There are also birds that remain in certain parts of the refuge that normally would not do so except under unusual circumstances. Heimo Korth, a friend and astute birder who has lived along the upper Coleen River in the refuge for almost three decades, told me he had observed Mallards even in the dead of winter on the headwaters of the Old Crow River. There is open water there, he said, and if ducks can eat there all year, they'll stick around. He also told me a story about a White-crowned Sparrow that somehow failed to migrate and hung around his cabin until midwinter. It hid under the cabin at night and would come out to feed during the short daylight hours. Heimo had killed a grizzly bear and left the carcass in the snow nearby, and every morning he would watch the fluffy-feathered bird emerge from the hole under the cabin, alight on the carcass, and eat the fat from the meat. One day, though, he didn't

see the little sparrow, and he understood why when he investigated and found weasel tracks entering the hole.

The refuge stretches from the Beaufort Sea to well south of the Porcupine River. This span in latitude, encompassing a broad variety of habitats and six distinct ecoregions, influences which species can survive and even flourish here during the winter, and it boils down to what food is available for them

Common Raven

under the difficult weather conditions with which they must contend. Since the northern portion of the refuge, including the coastal plain and the mountainous regions, is subject to the harshest weather and has virtually no tall trees, it has the fewest number of both species and individual birds that overwinter. The southern part of the refuge, however, is more benign, with less wind and more tree cover. There are more winter birds here as a result and, if my dream is any indication, more firewood for avian campfires.

Since many of the twenty-six winter species in my dream are covered elsewhere in this book, I've selected ten to discuss here that I regard as especially interesting or with which I've had personal encounters.

CHICKADEES

I'll begin with a wee bird I saw for the first time in June of 2004, on a rafting trip on the Marsh Fork of the Canning River in the northwest corner of the refuge. Our charter was late bringing in our raft, so I suggested to two friends that we take a short walk downriver to a heavily willowed outwash punctuated in places with sparse stands of cottonwood. I'd heard that Gray-headed Chickadees often nested in the cottonwoods and thought we might be lucky enough to spot one of these elusive birds.

We thrashed through thick willows for more than an hour and were just about to give up when I heard the definite *spish* of a chickadee. It was slower than that of Black-capped and Boreal Chickadees, but a chickadee it was. So I *spished* back and immediately spied it in the willows, poking around for insect tidbits. I glassed it to inspect its topknot and face, comparing it to the pictures of the chickadees in my bird guide. It did, in fact, have a grayer head than any of the Boreals I'd ever seen, and its white cheek patch was larger than that of the Boreal or Black-capped Chickadees. Finally, after hearing so much about this bird for so long, I was able to observe it up close and personal. When I *spished* again, it flew down right in front of me and ogled me as though I might have something to offer it.

Another began calling nearby. Its slow and easy *spish* was identical to the one I was trailing through the willows. Unfortunately, I couldn't spend all day following them; it was hot in that breezeless jungle, and I didn't want to alienate my friends with my enthusiasm. As I pushed through the willows onto the open tundra, I stopped to listen to the chickadees one last time. *Tsiti ti ti jeew . . . jeew jeew.* Then they stopped, and that was the last time I heard their call.

This hardy bird is the rarest and least understood of our North American chickadees. It is an Old World bird, known as the Siberian Tit in northern Russia and Europe, that crossed the Bering Strait during one of the last glaciations and established itself in the northern part of the continent to as far east as the Mackenzie River valley in Canada. It is a permanent resident found at or north of the tree line where stunted spruces, cottonwoods, and willows grow along remote Arctic creeks and rivers such as the Canning, Kongakut, and Clarence Rivers. Like other chickadee species, it feeds in small family groups on insects, larvae, spiders, seeds, and the fat of dead animals. Its foraging strategies, too, are similar to those of other chickadees, including the storage of food for later retrieval.

Once mated, Gray-headed Chickadees remain together all year on a large permanent territory that may be shared by one other mated pair. They nest in tree cavities, usually in dead or dying spruce or cottonwood trees. The nest, built by the female, is made of grass, moss, and animal hair. The male feeds the female as part of their mating ritual and continues to do so throughout the incubation period and until the nestlings are about half-grown. Between four and eleven white, reddish brown spotted eggs are laid, and incubation is done totally by the female, for fourteen to eighteen days. After the eggs hatch, the female broods the young most of the time at first while the male brings food. Later both parents share these duties. The young leave the nest when they are about twenty days old. Heimo and I both think it's likely that pairs that nest on the north side of the Brooks Range migrate along with their offspring to the more heavily wooded southern side of the mountains during the cold winter months.

Of the Gray-headed Chickadee's two cousins, the Black-capped and Boreal Chickadees, the Boreal Chickadee is probably the most common of all the winter birds in the refuge, especially where there are spruce trees.

Until I met the Gray-headed Chickadees, I always thought of boreals as country cousins of black-caps. Compared to the calls of black-caps and others that range far to the south, the slow, almost drawling *spish* of a boreal is a fascination. I love to listen to them in the forest, and when I *spish* back they immediately come over to investigate. In the fall I've had a dozen of them surround me, wondering where the noise was coming from.

Like other chickadee species, boreals feed on insects, spiders, seeds, and animal fat. They are monogamous, possibly mate for life, and remain together in the same general area all year. Their mating ritual usually starts in the top of a spruce: The male chases the female in a downward spiral around the tree. Mating occurs after sweet solicitation calls by the female during which she also asks for food from the male.

Boreals nest in the holes of trees, usually in either a natural cavity or one hacked out by woodpeckers, although they also will dig their own. Both male and female help with the excavation, but only the female builds the nest inside, using moss, feathers, animal hair, and plant down. As many as nine white, reddish brown dotted eggs are laid, and only the female incubates them. During the eleven- to sixteen-day incubation period the male feeds his mate. After the eggs hatch, the female stays home to brood the young while her mate works very hard to bring home the bacon. Both adults feed the nestlings as they grow larger until finally, at about eighteen days, the young fledge and learn to provide for themselves, foraging for food rich in carbohydrates and storing much of it for retrieval during the winter.

But winter nights are so long in the Arctic Refuge that boreals and other chickadee species have to do more than simply get fat on rich foods in order to survive. To get through those frigid, foodless nights they roost in tree cavities in a state of "regulated hypothermia," in which their body temperature drops as much as twenty degrees F below their normal daytime body temperature. As a result, they don't have to expend as much energy, stored in fat reserves, to heat their bodies. They also have other cold-weather adaptations: By shivering their muscles, they use stored fat reserves to generate heat and to regulate their body temperature when cooling down at night. They also have denser plumage than southern birds their size, a trait that doesn't make for the most graceful flying but provides the insulation they need to successfully survive Arctic winters.

CROSSBILLS

According to my friend Heimo, the next most common winter bird in his part of the refuge is the White-winged Crossbill. But this northern crossbill has been known to leave the area on a moment's notice. In fact, if the spruce and tamarack cone seed crop upon which they feed is not abundant, they will wander, often in large flocks, throughout the boreal zones of the Northern Hemisphere in search of trees heavily laden with cones. They may even travel far into Canada or south to Fairbanks, as they did a few years ago. When they find such crops they may settle in the area for a while, even building nests and raising young in the middle of winter.

Crossbills have one of the most unusual beaks in the bird world. Ogle the beak through your binocs and it appears almost deformed. But watch a crossbill perform up at the top of a tree with a spruce or tamarack cone in its grasp and you'll see that the beak is perfectly adapted to pry open the cones, allowing it to extract the seeds with its dexterous tongue.

No matter the time of year, if the seed crop is particularly good, a flock of these tough little birds may collectively decide to go into nesting mode. You'll be able to tell by a change in their behavior and the sound of their song. In their courtship flight, the male changes his tone from a sharp, metallic *cheet* to a continuous sweet twitter similar to that of a redpoll. He beats his wings slowly as he circles above the female, sometimes chasing her in the air. The pair may perch close together, touching beaks, and the male often feeds his mate. They nest high up on the horizontal limbs of spruces, and the nest is an open cup of twigs and grass, lined with moss, hair, and soft plant fiber. It is built by the female, although the male may help by bringing nesting materials. Four spotted, pale bluish green to white eggs are laid, and the female incubates them for about two weeks while her mate provides her with regurgitated seeds. After feeding her, he occasionally will give a flight-song display. When the eggs hatch, the female broods the young while the male brings food, this time in the form of a regurgitant of milky seed pulp. As the nestlings grow bigger, both parents feed them until about a fortnight after hatching, when they leave the nest. If the female begins another brood, her mate will attend the first batch of fledglings until they're totally on their own.

An important adaptation that allows crossbills to survive the severe refuge winters is an enlarged crop known as a gular pouch. They store extra seeds in the gular pouch as they eat, especially toward nightfall and at the onset of inclement weather. This "lunch box" of extra food will carry the birds through the night and the cold by allowing them to slowly digest while resting in a sheltered spot. Another way they cope with the Arctic cold is by growing more down feathers in the fall and fluffing up these feathers as they remain completely still in their snow-enclosed spruce shelters.

PTARMIGAN

Two much larger birds that prepare themselves for winter in the refuge with similar adaptations are members of the grouse family: Rock and Willow Ptarmigan. These birds not only grow very thick, downy body plumage to hold in warmth, but their feet are also heavily feathered to the tips of their sharp claws and act as snowshoes to allow them to walk more easily on the surface of the snow. On cold winter nights they burrow into the snow to sleep, allowing the insulating value of the snow to keep them warm. Like crossbills and other winter finches, they, too, have a gular pouch in which they store food for digestion during the night or a winter snowstorm.

Inupiat Eskimos who live on the edge of the refuge call Willow and Rock Ptarmigan *Kadgivik* and *Niksaktongik*, respectively. The name *Kadgivik* refers to the red comb over the eyes of the Willow Ptarmigan male that is raised conspicuously during courtship display. *Niksaktongik* relates to the loud belching noise the Rock Ptarmigan makes when he is disturbed. I've surprised these birds on the tundra and mistaken the belch for the growl of a grizzly bear. You can imagine my reaction.

As the names of the birds indicate, they occupy somewhat different habitats in the Arctic Refuge. While Rock Ptarmigan prefer the tundra of the coastal plain and the alpine zone of the Brooks Range, Willow Ptarmigan—well, they really do prefer the willows. However, there is much overlap, especially on the coastal plain, where I've seen both species nesting near each other on the Okerokovik River, not far from the Beaufort Sea.

These two ptarmigan species subsist on similar diets of buds, leaves, and seeds of willows, alder, and dwarf birch. They also eat crowberries, blueberries, and cranberries, plus insects and spiders. When the chicks are young they at first feed heavily on insects, gradually eating more and more plant material.

It's a real treat to watch the male birds of these species perform during the mating season. Sometimes it's hard to tell whether their behavior is intended to frighten away other males or to attract females. The way they raise their nuptial

Rock Ptarmigan

eyebrows, throw their heads back, fan their tails, and strut proudly around their nesting ground is a sight to behold. And that's not all; they follow this activity by taking flight, rapidly flapping their wings, gliding, then fluttering back down to the ground as they utter their own macho version of a guttural croak.

The two species build their nests on the ground in a similar manner, although Rock Ptarmigan prefer a somewhat more open and, yes, rocky area. The females of both species build these nests in a shallow depression and line them with grass, leaves, moss, and feathers. They each often lay more than a dozen pale brown-splotched eggs and incubate them alone for about three weeks. Unlike other species of ptarmigan, the male Willow Ptarmigan remains close to the female throughout the incubation period. Hiding in a thicket near the nest, he will do whatever it takes to defend his mate from attacks by gulls and jaegers, even knocking them over to prevent them from getting the eggs. One male was documented to even have attacked a grizzly bear that stumbled into his mate's nest.

All of the eggs of the two species hatch at roughly the same time, and within just a few hours the downy chicks leave the nest with their mother and begin foraging on their own. The female tends the young and broods them while they are still small, but within two weeks the young can fly well enough to escape land predators, and by the end of the summer they are independent of their parents.

Because winter winds and temperatures are so harsh on the coastal plain of the refuge, both species gather in large flocks and move lower on the mountains and somewhat south of their breeding range at that time, although they normally do not go beyond the tree line.

SPRUCE GROUSE

Another hardy member of the grouse family that spends the winter in the Arctic Refuge is the Spruce Grouse. Somewhat uncommon, they are resident only on the south side of the refuge. A few years ago I was skiing in the forest

Immature Spruce Grouse

during late winter and noticed a spruce branch that appeared ragged and torn. On closer inspection I found the branch almost totally denuded of its needles. "Aha, Spruce Grouse," I thought, because spruce needles and buds are what these grouse eat in winter. This grouse has many other English names: Canada Grouse, Black Grouse, Cedar Partridge, Spotted Grouse, Spruce Partridge, Swamp Partridge, Wood Grouse, Wood Partridge, Spruce Hen, and Fool Hen. The last name comes from their habit of "freezing" on a low spruce tree limb as they are approached by humans. This makes them an easy target, and they have become a tasty supplement to the menu of Athabascan Indians living in the boreal forest near the Arctic Refuge.

I've found three scientific names for this bird. As with all species, only one scientific name is the "correct" one at any given time, although they are changed occasionally. The American Ornithologist's Union currently lists the scientific name as *Falcipennis canadensis*, although the one I prefer is *Canachites canadensis*, meaning "Canadian noisemaker." This refers to the noise the male makes during his territorial and mating displays in spring. On his nesting ground in the boreal forest of the refuge, usually alongside a fallen tree that has been used over many years for shelter, the male Spruce Grouse rapidly beats his wings together above his back while rising in the air and landing on the ground. As the female watches nearby, the male spreads his handsome, orange-tipped tail feathers, raises his bright red eyebrow combs, and makes a low hooting sound, trying his hardest to command her attention in the mating game.

Once mated, the female scratches out a shallow depression on the ground under dense cover; lines it with a few needles, grasses, and leaf litter; and then lays up to ten brown-blotched, buff- to olive-colored eggs. As with her ptarmigan cousins, she alone incubates the eggs, and after they hatch three weeks later, she also cares for the young. The chicks are precocial and leave the nest soon after they hatch. The downy hatchlings are immediately able to feed themselves, but at night and in cool weather their mother broods them to keep them warm. Within just a week the young are able to flutter up from the ground to low tree branches to escape predators such as foxes. To distract these predators, the mother bird performs a "broken-wing act," which almost always works.

WOODPECKERS

Among the huddle of winter birds around the campfire in my dream were four woodpeckers. Of these, the one most commonly found in the boreal forest of the Arctic Refuge is the American Three-toed Woodpecker. When my friend Heimo Korth and I were comparing notes on this bird, we both discovered we had often been able to coax them closer to us by tapping a twig against a tree trunk. Once, one landed so near and peered at me so intently that I could see a little spark of light reflecting from his left eyeball.

You'll find this woodpecker mostly in areas of the forest that have recently been burned by a forest fire. Big infestations of wood-boring insects concentrate in these areas, and three-toeds take full advantage of the bonanza. In healthy parts of the forest where there has been a population explosion of the spruce bark beetle, they often provide the most effective control of that major forest pest. Why they and their cousins, Black-backed Woodpeckers, have only three toes instead of the usual four that other birds have is a puzzle, but it certainly doesn't impede their chances of survival even in the harsh environment of the southern part of the Arctic Refuge. Heimo says both species of three-toed are present year round where he lives.

One of the survival strategies of the American Three-toed is a strong pair bond that lasts all year and sometimes continues over successive years. The male also assists the female in the excavation of the nest cavity, takes his turn with incubation (mostly at night), and helps feed and tend the nestlings after they hatch until well beyond the fledging period.

The nesting season begins with much tree drumming by the male, which both attracts females and informs other males of his territorial dominance. He also does a lot of head swaying and calls more loudly than usual. This usually does the trick, and it isn't long before four white eggs are laid in the nest. In two weeks these eggs hatch, and, since the chicks are altricial, it is more than three weeks until they hesitantly take their first flight from the nest cavity. It is another four to eight weeks before they are totally on their own.

Both species of three-toed woodpeckers found in the refuge probably evolved from the same original species because so many of their behaviors are the same or similar. And although their ranges overlap, they may have hostile exchanges where they meet. For this reason, one or the other predominates. In the boreal forest of the Arctic Refuge, it seems the American Three-toed Woodpecker is the more prevalent.

GRAY JAY

I was surprised when Heimo told me the Gray Jay was rather rare in his area. Nevertheless, it is present; a few years ago I even saw a young one out on the refuge coastal plain. The jay was probably just being his teenage self and exploring, but it was a long way for a forest bird to roam.

The Gray Jay is variously called Canada Jay, camp robber, Cinerous Crow, and Whiskey Jack, among other common names. The last name comes from the Cree Indian word *whiska-zhon-shish*, meaning "the little one that works at a fire," and relates to the jay's propensity to visit campfires for an easy handout. Cinerous comes from the Latin word *cinereus*, which means "ashes," referring to the black and gray plumage of the jay.

As a member of the Corvid, or crow, family, Gray Jays have one of the largest brains per body size in the animal world. They have long, soft, and silky plumage, especially in winter, which keeps them warm when temperatures plummet to sixty degrees below zero. Gray Jays cache large quantities of food during the warmer months for use in winter, using their gluey saliva to help stick pieces of food in bark crevices and other hiding places. They can even carry food with their feet, a trait rare among songbirds.

Like so many of their Corvid cousins, Gray Jays are monogamous, and mated pairs stay together year round and defend permanent territories. You might see them in winter, often accompanied by their most dominant young. The parents

drive this young bird away in early spring, however, when the urge to nest takes over. Since they are permanently bonded, Gray Jays don't have much of a courting ritual, and usually all you'll see is some feeding of the female by the male. As soon as you spot this courtship feeding, you know the pair is building a nest somewhere on the branch of a dense spruce close to the trunk. The nest is a bulky cup made of sticks, grass, and moss fastened together with spider silk. It is well insulated with fur and feather down to accommodate the pair's tendency to nest when there is still much snow on the ground and temperatures are as low as thirty degrees below zero.

After laying three or four grayish white eggs, the female alone does the incubation while her mate provides her with food. In three weeks the eggs hatch, and the mother bird broods the young while the male brings food to the

Black-backed Woodpecker

nest for everyone. Later, when the young have a few more feathers and are less vulnerable to the cold, both parents will forage for food and bring it back to the nestlings. After another three weeks or so the young are ready to take their first flight, but they remain with their parents for at least another month to learn a few more survival strategies. Then they are on their own, although, as I mentioned, the most dominant of the offspring usually hangs around all winter with its parents. This may be so that at least one of the young learns all of the tricks of survival its parents know to help survive this very harsh climate.

Gray Jays learn things so well that some Alaska Native cultures once believed they had special powers of perception and that they were even conscious of the world around them in the sense that many of their actions were intentional or premeditated. No wonder, for a bird with such a large brain.

COMMON RAVEN

Closely related to the Gray Jay, the Common Raven is the bird regarded as the most conscious of them all by Native people everywhere in Alaska. But don't let its moniker fool you; this is no common bird. As our largest passerine, it is thought to be perhaps the most intelligent and socially adept bird on earth. In addition to having more than two hundred different vocalizations and many dialects, it has been described as crafty, resourceful, and quick to learn and profit from experience. Among southern Yupik Eskimos, it was once believed ravens possessed a much higher quality of awareness, referred to as *cella*, relating them to *Cellamyua*, meaning "Great Spirit." Northern Inupiat Eskimos and Gwich'in people who live near the refuge also once held them in greater esteem.

For a bird that sometimes establishes lifelong ties with its mate, the raven

Common Raven / Opposite ■ Bird print in snow

goes through some elaborate courtship rituals. Watch carefully in early spring and you'll see the male fly wingtip-to-wingtip with the female and then peel off and dive like a Peregrine Falcon, often tumbling over and over in the air, not unlike humans who "fall head over heels in love." When perched on a limb, raven couples touch shoulders, preen each other's feathers, and touch bills as though kissing.

After the ritual aerobatics comes the serious business of nest building, often beginning even while there is still much snow on the ground and it is quite cold. Both sexes help construct the nest, which they build high on a sheltered cliff ledge or in a tall tree. The nests are made of broken branches lined with leaves, grass, moss, fur, and feathers, in that order. After laying four or five green brown-spotted eggs, the female alone incubates them while her mate feeds her on the nest. About three weeks later the eggs hatch and both parents fetch food and water for the nestlings, although the mother broods them at night and when it's cold. Since they are such large birds, raven young take a long time to grow to the point where they are ready to take wing. But finally, after five or six weeks, they stand on the verge of the cliff ledge where they were born and, with a little coaxing from their parents, take their first tentative flight.

Even when they're all safely out of the nest and in the air, these altricial young still must depend upon their elders for both food and the life skills that will allow them to live long lives. For a bird that can live as long as twenty-five years, they have much to learn, including how to forage, scavenge, and hunt cooperatively in groups; how to cache food, wheel and tumble in the air, court their mates, play with their peers, be sociable in their communal roosts, and even *quork* and *bell-croak* in their peculiar Arctic Refuge dialect. They must also learn to contend with the intense cold of Arctic Refuge winters. As with other northern birds that have to cope with these frigid temperatures, ravens, too, have adaptive equipment that allows them to do this efficiently. In autumn they grow more down feathers, which they fluff up to add even more insulation. They put on additional body fat, are equipped with that lunch box called a gular pouch, and are blessed with an extraordinary circulatory system, which, along with muscle twitching and their signature cold-weather crouch, guarantees their lanky legs and feet will be around to see the light of another very short day. I can't help but think that the soft murmurings I've heard at their winter nocturnal roosts, much like the commiserations of humans, also help them get through these bitterly cold nights.

■ ■ ■

When I close my eyes to conjure up again the images of my campfire dream and the yellow flames flickering off the feathers and beaks of that motley crew of winter birds huddled around the fire, I am struck by the extraordinary differences in size, shape, color, behavior, and song. Although this may be so, they are every one kindred in their remarkable ability to survive in a climate where scant numbers of people have ever chosen to make their own home. Except for small groups of hardy Native Americans and a few non-Natives such as Heimo Korth, humans have not made much of a mark on the lives of the birds in what is now the Arctic National Wildlife Refuge. I fervently hope we never will. ■

Autumn Bird Research in the Arctic Refuge by Robin Hunnewell

Semipalmated Sandpiper

*T*he Okpilak River flows north across the Arctic coastal plain and empties into the Beaufort Sea. At its mouth it joins with the Hulahula River and forms a wide delta of swift channels that braid over tidal flats to a lagoon. Far to the south, in the Romanzof Mountains, is the Okpilak Glacier and moraine. From here a flour of sediment infuses the Okpilak so that its outflow carries plumes the color of milk chocolate far out to sea.

It is late summer, and the polar days have begun to admit an hour or two of twilight, foreshadowing the coming of winter. At this time of year the river deltas are habitat for shorebirds that will soon migrate to wintering grounds in the Southern Hemisphere. Their layover here is timed to coincide with blooms of invertebrate life on the tidal flats, staging for flights that follow the curvature of the earth over two continents. As a strategy for survival, it seems as improbable as any in the natural world, but it is fueled by full-blown necessity.

By comparison, fieldwork in the Arctic is unadventurous. Our team is here to conduct research on the post-breeding movements of shorebirds in the Arctic Refuge. We are stationed on the delta of the Okpilak River, and our study plans include spatial monitoring of birds moving within and among river deltas of the Arctic coast. The goal: to track how shorebirds make use of the time and space given to them as they prepare for their southward migrations. In order to follow them we must catch, band, and fit radios to the birds, and then listen for their signals. Catching shorebirds means finding them in large enough gatherings to make our light mist nets effective.

We set upright mist nets on the flats in opportune areas where birds are foraging into the wind. We wait. When it is calm, the quiet is complete except for the restless calls of shorebirds. Now and then there is the low boom of ice shifting outside the lagoon. When there is wind, the air shakes with the roar of surf, and the weather changes rapidly. We are warm and enveloped in insects one moment and then plunged into fog and bitter cold the next.

When a parade of young Semipalmated Sandpipers appears in the sunlit fog before us, we watch intently. They thrust their bills to the hilt in the watery mud and are lost in a dazzling blur. If our proximity is not tolerated, a quick lift of the wings will take them banking away.

A shout goes up, announcing a capture! We sprint to the net and carefully extract a sandpiper from the soft mesh. We band the bird, measure it, equip it with a small radio, and then release it. As a tiny beacon of information, it will now relay valuable clues about itself, its species, and the Arctic Refuge, helping us to preserve its habitats—and its future. ■

and their habitats are not entirely certain, but for the wildlife of the Arctic coastal plain, the changes cannot be good.

A primary concern as it relates to interactions between global warming and petroleum development is shifting vegetation zones. Rising temperatures encourage the growth of taller, denser, woody vegetation. Boreal forests will extend north, and areas that are now vegetated by fine grasses and sedges will be invaded by willows. This is a fundamental problem for the birds that nest, molt, and stage on the open tundra of the Arctic coastal plain. Taller, woody vegetation conceals predators, reduces the extent of nesting habitats, and may change the composition and availability of insects and other foods. At the same time, the physical extent of the coastal plain may simply shrink due to coastal erosion from the rise in sea level.

If vast oilfield complexes are superimposed on this already-changing landscape, whether in the Arctic Refuge or in the NPR-A to the west, it is easy to foresee that habitat available for the birds of the coastal plain will shrink and be degraded. Birds with more specialized habitat requirements, such as molting geese in the area north of Teshekpuk Lake, will suffer the most. Reduced populations and conceivably the extinction of some species whose populations already are small may follow.

PROTECTED AREAS

Given the certainty of North Slope ecological change induced by global warming and the continued expansion of the petroleum development, there is a need to identify ways to avoid, reduce, or mitigate negative effects. Planning for ecological change, however, requires an understanding of the sources and nature of the changes, which is complicated by the lack of a system of scientific control areas—free or largely free of the influence of petroleum development—across the North Slope. It will be difficult, if not impossible, to tease apart the effects of global warming and the petroleum industry when there are no sizeable areas free of oil and gas activity.

At present, there is a single Long Term Ecological Research site established by the National Science Foundation at Toolik Lake, which is in the foothills of the Brooks Range more than a hundred miles south of Prudhoe Bay. In its 2003 assessment, "The Cumulative Environmental Effects of Oil and Gas Activities on Alaska's North Slope," the National Research Council recommended establishment of similar protected areas in comparable areas within and outside industrial zones across the North Slope.

The possibility of seeing oilfield infrastructure across the entire North Slope coast, both on- and offshore, underscores the fact that there is no strategy in place for a network of even representative protected control areas—to say nothing of large-scale wilderness—in the Arctic. It also underscores the paramount importance of the opportunity for landscape-scale conservation in the Arctic Refuge and its coastal plain. The coastal plain of the Arctic Refuge—most of which is proposed for leasing by the Bush Administration—may be the best, if not the only, chance to preserve a significant portion of this ecoregion and to do so as part of a larger, wild Arctic ecosystem.

Common Ravens and nest

Tundra Swans, Prudhoe Bay   /   Opposite ■ Industrial infrastructure on coastal tundra, Prudhoe Bay

Photo: John Schoen

STAN SENNER *is executive director and vice president of Audubon Alaska. He has more than thirty years of experience in ornithology and in the fields of natural resources and wildlife conservation policy. Senner served as the science coordinator for the Anchorage-based* Exxon Valdez Oil Spill Trustee Council. ■

have been a low point—it certainly was a tense one—but Carolyn left her meeting with Congressman Bevill thinking, "Oh, wow—I can really use this in the future. It helps me understand how to organize and that it is never too early to organize." Carolyn immediately contacted all ten of the Sierra Club members in Representative Bevill's district and held a workshop on how to lobby, and devised a phone-tree to generate calls and letters in support of the Alaska Lands Act.

According to Carolyn, the connection between being a bird watcher and working to protect the Arctic is the easiest connection in the world to make. The most obvious connection is that a majority of the birds people love to watch are migratory. The next connection is the realization of the importance of protecting the Arctic habitat for these precious summer residents. In describing the importance of the Alaska Lands Act, all Carolyn had to do was show folks pictures of the Copper River Delta and the birds that fly there. As Carolyn says, in her endearing southern accent, "It really becomes very immediate, even though it's far away." And, she continued, you know that "birders are always talking about where the birds are going or coming from." Carolyn even knows a local Republican politician whose bird watching led to getting involved in protecting the environment. The politician became disappointed in her party's lack of conservation ethic, so she switched parties and became a Democrat.

Another connection that Carolyn has observed over the years is one between protecting the distant Arctic habitat to becoming actively involved in saving habitat locally—perhaps a reverse NIMBY (Not in My Backyard). Birders who devote their time and energy to protecting the distant habitat in the Arctic Refuge for the migrating birds may become even more committed to ensuring that the local stopping grounds also remain pristine. One of Carolyn's relatives, an avid birder, has become increasingly active over the years. "Can you picture it," Carolyn asks, "a grandmamma in her sixties leading a picketing group regarding a local land-use problem?" She never would have gotten involved if she hadn't been a birder.

■ ■ ■

All bird watchers, regardless of age, size, or field marks, have the necessary skills to be effective Arctic activists. It's a simple and logical step to extend birding skills to the campaign to protect the coastal plain of the Arctic National Wildlife Refuge.

Patience: Birders can wait indefinitely for that one unique warbler. Activists patiently apply endless pressure as they urge decision makers to vote to protect the Arctic.

Keen sense of observation: Birders observe the broader landscape for signs of potential bird activity, and they observe minute details of each bird to determine the species. Activists observe the political landscape for each member of Congress and observe what influences each member of Congress in choosing how to vote.

Listener: Birders can identify a bird by song. Activists listen and learn from their opponents.

Committed: Once they get started, birders are committed throughout their lifetime to getting up early, going where necessary, and doing what it takes to see that unique bird. Activists are committed to doing all it takes, from making phone calls to traveling to Washington, D.C., to protect the Arctic.

Flock together: Birders tend to bird in flocks, and birders flock together when a special bird is spotted. Activists know that in order to win the campaign to protect the Arctic, the flock has to grow.

■ ■ ■

As a bird lover and watcher, you already are an Arctic activist. Now take the next step: Contact your local conservation group and join up with the thousands of Americans who work to protect the Arctic National Wildlife Refuge.

CYNTHIA D. SHOGAN *is the executive director of the Alaska Wilderness League, which works to further the protection of Alaska's incomparable natural endowment through legislative and administrative activities, public education, and grass roots activism. In 2002 the Alaska Wilderness League was one of seven organizations to receive the inaugural Leadership Award from the Natural Resources Council of America for the environmental community's campaign to protect the Arctic National Wildlife Refuge. Shogan received the Wilburforce Foundation's Conservation Leadership Award in 2003.* ■

Opposite ■ *Canning River, Arctic National Wildlife Refuge*

All photographs were taken in the Arctic National Wildlife Refuge except as noted in parentheses.

Born in India in 1967, SUBHANKAR BANERJEE received his bachelor's degree in engineering before moving to the United States, where he obtained master's degrees in physics and computer science. Before starting his career in photography, Banerjee worked in the scientific fields for six years, with Los Alamos National Lab in New Mexico and Boeing in Seattle. His first professional photographic project culminated in a book, *Arctic National Wildlife Refuge: Seasons of Life and Land*, published by The Mountaineers Books. Solo exhibits of Banerjee's Arctic Refuge photographs have been on display at the Smithsonian National Museum of Natural History in Washington, American Museum of Natural History in New York, California Academy of Sciences in San Francisco, The Field Museum in Chicago, Burke Museum of Natural History and Culture in Seattle, Grand Rapids Art Museum in Grand Rapids, Museum of Utah Art and History in Salt Lake City, Gerald Peters Gallery in New York and Santa Fe, Wilding Art Museum in California, and other venues. Banerjee's photographs are represented exclusively by the Gerald Peters Gallery, Santa Fe–New York.

Photo credits: back cover and pages 8, 9, 19 (lower), 24–25, 28, 35, 41, 42 (lower), 53 (lower), 56–57, 59, 61, 64, 65 (left and right), 84 (lower), 86, 87, 91, 92–93, 107, 110–111, 128–129, 148–149, 153, 162–163, 168, 171, 173, 174, 176 (upper), 177, 179 (lower)

Growing up the son of an ice cream store owner and a schoolteacher in Valley Stream, New York, STEVE KAZLOWSKI craved a life pursuing nature. After earning a degree in marine biology from Towson University in Baltimore, he worked briefly for a marine lab before setting aside a microscope and picking up his camera. He headed to Alaska to become a wildlife photographer, initially working construction jobs and on fishing boats to support his dream. Kazlowski now works full time as an independent photographer. His images have been featured in *Audubon, Backpacking, Canadian National Geographic,* and *Time* magazines. Three books exclusively feature his photography: *Alaska Wildlife Impressions* (Farcountry Press, 2004), *Alaska Wildlife of the North* (Hancock House Publishing, 2005), and *Alaska Bears of the North* (Hancock House Publishing, 2005). He produces and distributes his own postcards and other print photographs, including via his website: *www.lefteyepro.com.* He resides in Seattle, Washington, in the winter and travels Alaska and the northeast throughout the year.

Photo credits: pages 1, 2–3 (central Arctic coast), 7, 12, 34, 36, 37, 39 (central Arctic coast), 42 (upper), 43, 44 (Interior Alaska), 46 (central Arctic coast), 47 (central Arctic coast), 49, 50 (left and right), 51, 52 (central Arctic coast), 53 (upper), 55, 62 (central Arctic coast), 67 (Denali National Park, Alaska), 68 (Kachemak Bay, south-central Alaska), 69 (upper and lower; both central Arctic coast), 78 (Semipalmated Plover), 80, 82 (Yukon, Canada), 83 (Wrangell-St. Elias National Park, Alaska), 88, 89, 90 (central Arctic coast), 96 (lower), 97 (lower), 101 (central Arctic coast), 102, 103, 108 (left and right), 109 (Kenai Fjords National Park, Alaska), 113 (Anchorage), 117, 118 (left; central Arctic coast), 126–127 (central Arctic coast), 138, 139, 144 (Denali National Park, Alaska), 146, 147 (left), 151, 153, 154 (Kenai Peninsula), 155 (Kenai Peninsula), 159 (lower), 165, 166, 176 (lower; Prudhoe Bay, Deadhorse, Alaska), 181

MICHIO HOSHINO was born in Ichikawa City, Japan, in 1952. At the age of seventeen, a photo of an Eskimo village on the northwest coast of Alaska in a National Geographic magazine inspired him to explore the vast wilderness. During the summer of 1972 he traveled to Shishmaref, Alaska, to live with the town's mayor. Hoshino returned to Japan and went on to major in economics at Keio University. In 1978 he left his native Japan to live in Alaska, where he studied wildlife management at the University of Alaska. His professional career as a photographer began with the publication of *Grizzly* (Chronicle Books, 1986), which won an Anima award for distinguished wildlife photography. Other books of his photographic work include *Moose* (Chronicle Books, 1988) and *The Grizzly Bear Family Book* (North-South, 1994), a work for children. His photographs have been published in numerous American and international magazines. On August 6, 1996, at the age of 44, Hoshino was killed by a brown bear while sleeping in his tent during a photo expedition on the Kamchatka Peninsula, in eastern Russia. He is survived by his wife, Naoko, and his son, Shoma.

Photo credits: front cover and pages 45, 70–71, 79, 104, 115 (right), 121, 124, 125. All photographs © Michio Hoshino/Minden Pictures.

With more than 20,000 of his images in publication, ARTHUR MORRIS is widely recognized as the world's premier bird photographer. For eight seasons he counted shorebirds at Jamaica Bay Wildlife Refuge, Queens, New York for the International Shorebird Surveys. *Shorebirds: Beautiful Beachcombers* was his first book, and his book *The Art of Bird Photography* is the classic how-to work on the subject. He is a popular *Photography* magazine columnist. Morris has been a Canon contract photographer for the past nine years. He currently travels, photographs, teaches, and speaks his way across North America while leading more than a dozen Birds as Art instructional photo tours each year.

Photo credits: pages 29 (Jamaica Bay Wildlife Refuge, New York), 31 (Nome, Alaska), 40 (Bosque Del Apache National Wildlife Refuge, New Mexico), 54 (Bosque Del Apache National Wildlife Refuge, New Mexico), 73 (Nome, Alaska), 75 (right; Barrow, Alaska), 95 (Nome, Alaska), 96 (upper; Nome, Alaska), 98 (Katmai National Park, Alaska), 99 (Nome, Alaska), 126 (left; Nome, Alaska), 131 (Nome, Alaska), 132 (lower; Churchill, Manitoba, Canada), 134 (upper; Churchill, Manitoba, Canada), 167 (Jamaica Bay Wildlife Refuge, New York), 170 (Point Pelee National Park, Ontario, Canada)

HUGH ROSE received his bachelor's and master's degrees in geology from the University of Vermont, and after a ten-year career in geology that included teaching and geologic mapping, he moved to Alaska to explore and photograph the Arctic wilderness. He worked as a naturalist guide in Denali National Park for six years and since then has guided natural history trips from Alaska to Antarctica and places in between. Hugh's travels have taken him to the Arctic National Wildlife Refuge in all seasons of the year, and the refuge remains one of the most remarkable places he has ever visited. "Of all the places I have visited on earth, the Arctic National Wildlife Refuge is the most special to me and continues to draw me back, time and again," says Rose. "I hope we can have enough foresight to not squander this valuable wilderness resource for the sake of six months' worth of oil. The wilderness value of the refuge far exceeds its oil value in the twenty-first century, where solitude and natural beauty are more rare than oil deposits."

Photo credits: pages 11, 20 (left and right), 30, 38, 63 (Brooks Range), 66, 75 (left), 78 (Lesser Yellowlegs), 85 (lower), 106, 115 (left; just outside the refuge), 116 (right), 120, 123, 132, 134, 140 (also CD image), 141, 143, 145, 147 (right), 156, 157, 158, 159 (upper), 160, 161, 164 (left and right), 169

MARK WILSON loves to travel in the wilderness by canoe because, as a photographer, he's inclined to bring a lot of heavy photo gear on trips. Wilson has returned to the Arctic over and over again, drawn by the amazing light, the incredible birds, and its great sense of space and time. He and his wife, Marcia, both naturalists and avid birders, offer slide programs about the Arctic that include bringing a Snowy Owl to audiences in New England. Wilson, who once took second place in a World Press competition for a photo of a Great Gray Owl, is a staff photographer at the *Boston Globe,* where he has worked for twenty years.

Photo credits: pages 15 (Arctic Alaska), 17 (all), 19 (upper), 21, 22, 23, 48, 60 (upper and lower), 78 (Baird's Sandpiper), 85 (upper), 116 (left), 118 (right), 119, 122, 136, 142, 179 (upper), 182

The Arctic National Wildlife Refuge is a vast and isolated landscape where birdlife has been largely unphotographed. Important gaps in documentation for Arctic Wings *were filled by contributors who took photographs while in the refuge for research or exploration. We are grateful for the use of their images.*

STEPHEN BROWN: pages 78 (Pectoral Sandpiper), 84 (upper), 97 (upper)
ROBIN HUNNEWELL: page 78 (American Golden-Plover)
DEBBIE MILLER: pages 33, 105, 133, 137 (upper and lower)
BRAD WINN: 76, 78 (Pectoral Sandpiper nest, American Golden-Plover nest), 81, 135

Birds of the Arctic National Wildlife Refuge

Courtesy of Steve Kendall, Wildlife Biologist, U.S. Fish and Wildlife Service, Arctic National Wildlife Refuge

There are currently 194 bird species officially documented as occurring in the Arctic National Wildlife Refuge. This list was compiled over decades by refuge biologists and dedicated volunteers. Because many areas of the refuge are rarely or infrequently visited, information about the occurrence, distribution, and breeding status of birds is incomplete. The list of species changes continuously as more birders and scientists visit the refuge and report on the birds using the area. This list is organized following the standard taxonomic order used in most bird guides. In the Breeding Status column, *B* indicates that the species has been documented to breed in the refuge, and *P* indicates that the species is a probable breeder in the refuge. Those species without a letter indicator in this column do not breed here but depend to some degree on the refuge for part of their life cycle, such as stopping over during migration between breeding and wintering areas.

—*Stephen Brown*

Common Name	Scientific Name	Breeding Status
Greater White-fronted Goose	Anser albifrons	B
Snow Goose	Chen caerulescens	
Ross's Goose	Chen rossii	
Brant	Branta bernicla	B
Cackling Goose (Taverner's)	Branta hutchinsii	B
Canada Goose (Lesser)	Branta canadensis	B
Trumpeter Swan	Cygnus buccinator	B
Tundra Swan	Cygnus columbianus	B
Gadwall	Anas strepera	
Eurasian Wigeon	Anas penelope	
American Wigeon	Anas americana	B
Mallard	Anas platyrhynchos	B
Northern Shoveler	Anas clypeata	P
Northern Pintail	Anas acuta	B
Green-winged Teal	Anas crecca	B
Canvasback	Aythya valisineria	
Redhead	Aythya americana	
Ring-necked Duck	Aythya collaris	
Greater Scaup	Aythya marila	B
Lesser Scaup	Aythya affinis	B
Steller's Eider	Polysticta stelleri	
Spectacled Eider	Somateria fischeri	B
King Eider	Somateria spectabilis	B
Common Eider	Somateria mollissima	B
Harlequin Duck	Histrionicus histrionicus	B
Surf Scoter	Melanitta perspicillata	P
White-winged Scoter	Melanitta fusca	P
Black Scoter	Melanitta nigra	
Long-tailed Duck	Clangula hyemalis	B
Bufflehead	Bucephala albeola	
Common Goldeneye	Bucephala clangula	P
Barrow's Goldeneye	Bucephala islandica	
Smew	Mergellus albellus	
Common Merganser	Mergus merganser	
Red-breasted Merganser	Mergus serrator	B
Ruffed Grouse	Bonasa umbellus	P
Spruce Grouse	Falcipennis canadensis	P
Willow Ptarmigan	Lagopus lagopus	B
Rock Ptarmigan	Lagopus muta	B
Sharp-tailed Grouse	Tympanuchus phasianellus	P
Red-throated Loon	Gavia stellata	B
Pacific Loon	Gavia pacifica	B
Common Loon	Gavia immer	
Yellow-billed Loon	Gavia adamsii	
Horned Grebe	Podiceps auritus	P
Red-necked Grebe	Podiceps grisegena	P
Northern Fulmar	Fulmarus glacialis	
Short-tailed Shearwater	Puffinus tenuirostris	
Osprey	Pandion haliaetus	
Bald Eagle	Haliaeetus leucocephalus	B
Northern Harrier	Circus cyaneus	B
Sharp-shinned Hawk	Accipiter striatus	P
Northern Goshawk	Accipiter gentilis	B
Swainson's Hawk	Buteo swainsoni	B
Red-tailed Hawk	Buteo jamaicensis	
Rough-legged Hawk	Buteo lagopus	B
Golden Eagle	Aquila chrysaetos	B
American Kestrel	Falco sparverius	B
Merlin	Falco columbarius	P
Gyrfalcon	Falco rusticolus	B
Peregrine Falcon	Falco peregrinus	B
American Coot	Fulica americana	
Sandhill Crane	Grus canadensis	B
Black-bellied Plover	Pluvialis squatarola	B
American Golden-Plover	Pluvialis dominica	B
Semipalmated Plover	Charadrius semipalmatus	B
Killdeer	Charadrius vociferus	
Eurasian Dotterel	Charadrius morinellus	
Lesser Yellowlegs	Tringa flavipes	B
Solitary Sandpiper	Tringa solitaria	P
Wandering Tattler	Heteroscelus incanus	B
Spotted Sandpiper	Actitis macularius	B
Upland Sandpiper	Bartramia longicauda	B
Whimbrel	Numenius phaeopus	B
Black-tailed Godwit	Limosa limosa	
Hudsonian Godwit	Limosa haemastica	
Bar-tailed Godwit	Limosa lapponica	P
Ruddy Turnstone	Arenaria interpres	B
Surfbird	Aphriza virgata	B
Red Knot	Calidris canutus	
Sanderling	Calidris alba	B
Semipalmated Sandpiper	Calidris pusilla	B
Western Sandpiper	Calidris mauri	P
Red-necked Stint	Calidris ruficollis	
Least Sandpiper	Calidris minutilla	B
White-rumped Sandpiper	Calidris fuscicollis	B
Baird's Sandpiper	Calidris bairdii	B
Pectoral Sandpiper	Calidris melanotos	B
Sharp-tailed Sandpiper	Calidris acuminata	
Dunlin	Calidris alpina	B
Stilt Sandpiper	Calidris himantopus	B
Buff-breasted Sandpiper	Tryngites subruficollis	B
Ruff	Philomachus pugnax	
Long-billed Dowitcher	Limnodromus scolopaceus	B
Wilson's Snipe	Gallinago delicata	B
Wilson's Phalarope	Phalaropus tricolor	
Red-necked Phalarope	Phalaropus lobatus	B
Red Phalarope	Phalaropus fulicarius	B
Pomarine Jaeger	Stercorarius pomarinus	B
Parasitic Jaeger	Stercorarius parasiticus	B
Long-tailed Jaeger	Stercorarius longicaudus	B
Bonaparte's Gull	Larus philadelphia	
Mew Gull	Larus canus	B
Herring Gull	Larus argentatus	B
Thayer's Gull	Larus thayeri	
Slaty-backed Gull	Larus schistisagus	
Glaucous-winged Gull	Larus glaucescens	
Glaucous Gull	Larus hyperboreus	B
Sabine's Gull	Xema sabini	B
Black-legged Kittiwake	Rissa tridactyla	
Ross's Gull	Rhodostethia rosea	
Ivory Gull	Pagophila eburnea	
Arctic Tern	Sterna paradisaea	B
Thick-billed Murre	Uria lomvia	
Black Guillemot	Cepphus grylle	B
Least Auklet	Aethia pusilla	
Horned Puffin	Fratercula corniculata	
Great Horned Owl	Bubo virginianus	
Snowy Owl	Bubo scandiacus	B
Northern Hawk Owl	Surnia ulula	B
Great Gray Owl	Strix nebulosa	P
Short-eared Owl	Asio flammeus	B
Boreal Owl	Aegolius funereus	P
Common Nighthawk	Chordeiles minor	
Ruby-throated Hummingbird	Archilochus colubris	
Rufous Hummingbird	Selasphorus rufus	
Belted Kingfisher	Ceryle alcyon	P
Downy Woodpecker	Picoides pubescens	P
Hairy Woodpecker	Picoides villosus	P
American Three-toed Woodpecker	Picoides dorsalis	B
Black-backed Woodpecker	Picoides arcticus	P
Northern Flicker	Colaptes auratus	B
Olive-sided Flycatcher	Contopus cooperi	
Alder Flycatcher	Empidonax alnorum	P
Hammond's Flycatcher	Empidonax hammondii	P
Eastern Phoebe	Sayornis phoebe	
Say's Phoebe	Sayornis saya	B
Eastern Kingbird	Tyrannus tyrannus	
Northern Shrike	Lanius excubitor	B
Gray Jay	Perisoreus canadensis	B
Common Raven	Corvus corax	B
Horned Lark	Eremophila alpestris	B
Tree Swallow	Tachycineta bicolor	
Violet-green Swallow	Tachycineta thalassina	B
Bank Swallow	Riparia riparia	P
Cliff Swallow	Petrochelidon pyrrhonota	B
Barn Swallow	Hirundo rustica	
Black-capped Chickadee	Poecile atricapillus	
Boreal Chickadee	Poecile hudsonica	B
Gray-headed Chickadee	Poecile cincta	B
Red-breasted Nuthatch	Sitta canadensis	
American Dipper	Cinclus mexicanus	B
Ruby-crowned Kinglet	Regulus calendula	B
Arctic Warbler	Phylloscopus borealis	B
Bluethroat	Luscinia svecica	B
Northern Wheatear	Oenanthe oenanthe	B
Townsend's Solitaire	Myadestes townsendi	
Gray-cheeked Thrush	Catharus minimus	B
Swainson's Thrush	Catharus ustulatus	P
Hermit Thrush	Catharus guttatus	
American Robin	Turdus migratorius	B
Varied Thrush	Ixoreus naevius	B
Eastern Yellow Wagtail	Motacilla tschutschensis	B
American Pipit	Anthus rubescens	B
Bohemian Waxwing	Bombycilla garrulus	B
Cedar Waxwing	Bombycilla cedrorum	
Orange-crowned Warbler	Vermivora celata	B
Yellow Warbler	Dendroica petechia	B
Yellow-rumped Warbler	Dendroica coronata	B
Blackpoll Warbler	Dendroica striata	P
Northern Waterthrush	Seiurus noveboracensis	P
Wilson's Warbler	Wilsonia pusilla	B
American Tree Sparrow	Spizella arborea	B
Chipping Sparrow	Spizella passerina	
Clay-colored Sparrow	Spizella pallida	
Savannah Sparrow	Passerculus sandwichensis	B
Fox Sparrow	Passerella iliaca	B
Lincoln's Sparrow	Melospiza lincolnii	
White-throated Sparrow	Zonotrichia albicollis	
White-crowned Sparrow	Zonotrichia leucophrys	B
Golden-crowned Sparrow	Zonotrichia atricapilla	B
Dark-eyed Junco	Junco hyemalis	B
Lapland Longspur	Calcarius lapponicus	B
Smith's Longspur	Calcarius pictus	B
Snow Bunting	Plectrophenax nivalis	B
Red-winged Blackbird	Agelaius phoeniceus	
Rusty Blackbird	Euphagus carolinus	B
Brown-headed Cowbird	Molothrus ater	
Gray-crowned Rosy-Finch	Leucosticte tephrocotis	B
Pine Grosbeak	Pinicola enucleator	B
White-winged Crossbill	Loxia leucoptera	B
Common Redpoll	Carduelis flammea	B
Hoary Redpoll	Carduelis hornemanni	B
Pine Siskin	Carduelis pinus	

Bird Index

Bold-faced page numbers indicate photographs